D0196589

WORKS OF BERTOLT BRECHT

The Grove Press Edition

General Editor: Eric Bentley

Translators

Lee Baxandall

Eric Bentley

Martin Esslin

N. Goold-Verschoyle

H. R. Hays

Anselm Hollo

Christopher Isherwood

Frank Jones

Charles Laughton

Carl R. Mueller

Desmond I. Vesey

BERTOLT BRECHT

MOTHER COURAGE
AND HER CHILDREN

A Chronicle of the Thirty Years' War

English version by
ERIC BENTLEY
*Complete and
unabridged edition*

GROVE PRESS
New York

Library of Congress Cataloging-in-Publication Data

Brecht, Bertolt, 1898-1956
       [Mutter Courage und ihre Kinder. English]
       Mother courage and her children: a chronicle of
the Thirty Years' War/Bertolt Brecht; English version
by Eric Bentley.—Complete and unabridged ed.

       Translation of: Mutter Courage und ihre Kinder.
       ISBN 0-8021-3082-8
PT2603.R397M82   1991
832'.914—dc20   91-761

Grove Press
841 Broadway
New York, NY 10003

02 03 04 05 06   40 39 38 37 36 35 34

Acknowledgment

I have been at work on the translating of *Mother Courage* since 1950. I have acknowledged the help I received in making the first two versions of it that I brought out. For this, the complete text, I received further help and counsel from Dr. Hugo Schmidt.

—E.B.
1963

CONTENTS

WHO IS MOTHER COURAGE?

The role is hard to play and is always being miscast.
Why? "Because middle-aged actresses are such ladies and
lack earthiness." But who has succeeded in the role? Out-
standingly, Helene Weigel. Is she very earthy, is she
notably proletarian? On the contrary—there is nothing proletarian about her except her opinions. Then what is it
those other ladies lack that Helene Weigel has? Among
other things, I would suggest: an appreciation of the role,
an understanding of what is in it, and above all the ability
to portray contradictions. For whenever anyone says,
"Mother Courage is essentially X" it is equally reasonable
for someone to retort: "Mother Courage is essentially the
exact opposite of X."

Mother Courage is essentially courageous. That is well-
known, isn't it? Mr. Tennessee Williams has written of the
final moment of Brecht's play as one of the inspiring moments in all theatre—inspiring because of the woman's
indomitability. On she marches with her wagon after all
that has happened, a symbol of the way humanity itself
goes on its way after all that has happened, *if* it can find
the courage. And after all we don't have to wait for the
final scene to learn that we have to deal with a woman of
considerable toughness and resilience. This is not the first
time she has shown that she can pick up the pieces and
continue. One might even find courage in the very first
scene where we learn that she has not been content to
cower in some corner of Bamberg but has boldly come to
meet the war. A trouble-shooter, we might say on first
meeting the lady, but the reverse of a coward.

Yet it is impossible to continue on this tack for long
without requiring an: *On the other hand.* Beginning with

9

the reason why she is nicknamed "Courage" in the first place.

> They call me Mother Courage because I was afraid I'd be ruined, so I drove through the bombardment of Riga like a madwoman with fifty loaves of bread in my cart. They were moldy, what else could I do?

Did those who gave her the name intend a joke against an obvious coward? Or did they think she was driven by heroic valor when in fact she was impelled by sheer necessity? Either way her act is utterly devoid of the moral quality imputed. Whether in cowardice or in down-to-earth realism, her stance is Falstaffian. What is courage? A word.

Somewhere hovering over this play is the image of a pre-eminently courageous mother who courageously tries to hold on to her young. More than one actress, offering herself for the role, has seen this image and nothing else. Yet valor is conspicuously absent at those times when Mother Courage (however unwittingly) seals the fate of her children. At moments when, in heroic melodrama, the protagonist would be riding to the rescue, come hell or high water, Mother Courage is in the back room concluding a little deal. For her, it is emphatically not "a time for greatness." *She is essentially cowardly*.

A basic contradiction, then, which the actress in the role must play both sides of, or the play will become the flat and simple thing which not a few journalistic commentators have declared it to be. An actress may be said to be beginning to play Mother Courage when she is putting both courage and cowardice into the role with equal conviction and equal effect. She is still only beginning to play it, though; for, as she proceeds with her interpretation, she will find that, in this play, courage and cowardice are not inherent and invariable qualities but by-products.

Of what? We can hunt for the answer by looking further into particular sequences of action. It is not really from cowardice that Mother Courage is in the back room concluding a little deal when her children are claimed by the war. It is from preoccupation with "business." Although *Mother Courage* is spoken of as a war play, it is actually a business play, in the sense that the incidents in it, one and all, are business transactions—from the deal with the belt in Scene One, through the deal with the capon in Scene Two, the deal with the wagon in Scene Three, the deals with bullets and shirts in Scene Five, through to the economical funeral arrangements of the final scene. And since these transactions (except for the last) are what Courage supports her children by, they are "necessary." Those who condemn her have to face the question: what alternative had she? Of what use would it have been to save the life of Swiss Cheese if she lacked the wherewithal to *keep* him alive? The severe judge will answer that she could take a chance on this, provided she does save his life. But this is exactly Mother Courage's own position. She is fully prepared to take the chance if she has to. It is in determining whether she has to that her boy's life slips through her fingers: life or death is a matter of timing.

To say that Swiss Cheese is a victim of circumstances, not of Courage's character, will not, however, be of much use to the actress interpreting this character. If cowardice is *less* important here than at first appears, what is *more* important? Surely it is a failure in understanding, rather than in virtue. Let me elaborate.

Though only one of Brecht's completed plays is about anyone that a university would recognize as a philosopher, several of his plays present what one might call philosophers in disguise, such as Schweyk, the philosopher of a pub in Prague, and Azdak, the philosopher of a Georgian village. To my mind, *Mother Courage is above all a philosopher,* defining the philosopher along Socratic lines as a person who likes to talk all the time and explain everything to everybody. (A simple trait in itself, one would think, yet there have been actresses and directors who wish to have all Courage's speeches shortened into mere remarks. But your philosopher never makes remarks; he always speechifies; hence such abridgement enforces a radical misinterpretation of character.) I do not mean at all that Courage is an idle or armchair philosopher whose teachings make no contact with life. On the contrary, her ideas are nothing if not a scheme of life by which, she hopes, her family is to do pretty well in a world which is doing pretty badly.

Here one sees the danger of thinking of Mother Courage as the average person. Rather, she resembles the thoughtfully ambitious modern mother of the lower-middle or better-paid working class who wants her children to win scholarships and end up in the Labour Cabinet. (Minister of Education: Kattrin. Chancellor of the Exchequer: Swiss Cheese. Minister of War: Eilif.)* Has it escaped attention that if one of her children turns out a cutthroat, this is blamed on circumstances ("Otherwise, I'd have starved, smarty"), while *the other two are outright heroes?* Anyone who considers this an average family takes a far higher view of the average than is implicit in the works of Bertolt Brecht.

What is the philosophy of this philosopher? Reduced to a single proposition, it is that if you concede defeat on the larger issue, you can achieve some nice victories in smaller ways. The larger issue is whether the world can be changed. It can't. But brandy is still drunk, and can be sold. One can survive, and one can help one's children to survive by teaching each to make appropriate use of the qualities God gave him. The proposition I have just mentioned will apply to this upbringing. A child endowed with a particular talent or virtue should not pursue it to its logical end: defeat on such projects should be conceded at the outset. The child should cunningly exploit his characteristic talent for its incidental uses along the way. In this fashion the unselfishness of a Swiss Cheese or a Kattrin can be harnessed to selfishness. The result, if the philosophy works, is that while the world may shoot itself to blazes, the little Courage family, one and all, will live out its days in

---

* The present essay was originally written for the program of *Mother Courage* at The National Theatre, London, 1965.

moderate wealth and moderate happiness. The scheme is not utopian. Just the opposite: the hope is to make optimism rational by reducing human demands to size.

The main reason it doesn't work is that the little world which Mother Courage's wisdom tries to regulate is dependent upon the big world which she has given up as a bad job. Small business is part of the big war which is part of the big business of ownership of *all* the means of production and distribution. No more than the small businessman can live in a separate economic system from the big, can the small philosopher live in a separate philosophic system from the big. *Mother Courage,* one can conclude, exposes the perennial illusions of the petit bourgeois scheme of things. This has of course often been done before in modern literature. But usually only the idealism has been exposed. Mother Courage, on the other hand, could claim to be a cynic. She has the theatre audience laughing most of the time on the score of this cynicism— by which *she* deflates illusions. Cynicism is nothing, after all, if not "realistic." What a cynical remark lays bare *has* to be the truth. Brecht makes the truth of his play the more poignant through the fact that the cynicism in it ultimately favors illusion. Mother Courage had gone to all lengths to trim her sails to the wind but even then the ship wouldn't move. So there is irony within irony (as, in Brecht's work, there usually is). Courage's cynicism can cut down the windy moralizing of the Chaplain easily enough, but only to be itself cut down by a world that cannot be comprehended even by this drastically skeptical kind of thinking.

What alternative did Mother Courage have? The only alternatives shown in the play are, on the one hand, the total brutalization of men like the Swedish Commander (and, for that matter, her own son Eilif) and, on the other hand, the martyrdom achieved by Swiss Cheese and Kattrin. Presumably, to the degree that the playwright criticizes her, he is pushing her toward the second alternative. Yet, not only would such a destiny be completely out of character, within the terms of the play itself it is not shown to be really preferable. Rather, the fruitlessness of both deaths is underlined. Why add a third?

Given her character, Mother Courage had no alternative to what she thought—or, for that matter, to the various "bad" things she did. In this case, can she be condemned? Logically, obviously not; but was Brecht logical? The printed editions of the play indicate that he made changes in his script to render Mother Courage less sympathetic. In other words, after having made her thoroughly sympathetic in his first version, Brecht later wanted her less so. One can see the sense of the changes in polemical terms: he did not wish to seem to condone behavior which is to be deplored. But to make this point, is it necessary to make Mother Courage a less good person? Personally I would think not, and I should like to see *Courage* played sometime in the Urtext of 1940 and without the later "improvements." But one should not minimize the complexity of the problem. Like many other playwrights, Brecht wanted to show a kind of inevitability combined with a degree of free will, and if it doesn't matter whether Courage is less good or more, because she is trapped by circumstances, then the play is fatalistic. I tend to think it *is* fatalistic as far as the movement of history is concerned, and that the element of hope in it springs only from Brecht's rendering of human character. Brecht himself is not satisfied with this and made changes in the hope of suggesting that things might have been different had Mother Courage acted otherwise. (What would she have done? Established Socialism in seventeenth-century Germany? One must not ask.)

Brecht has stressed, in his Notes, that Mother Courage never sees the light, never realizes what has happened, is incapable of learning. As usual, Brecht's opinions, as stated in outside comments, are more doctrinaire than those to be found embodied in the plays. It may be true that Mother Courage never sees that "small business" is a hopeless case, though to prove even this Brecht had to manufacture the evidence by inserting, later, the line at the end: "I must get back into business." She does see through her own philosophy of education. The "Song of Solomon" in Scene Nine concedes that the program announced in Scene One has failed. The manipulation of the virtues has not worked: "a man is better off without." The song is perhaps more symbolic, as well as more schematic, than most Brechtians wish Brecht to be, for there is a verse about each of her children under the form of famous men (Eilif is Caesar, Swiss Cheese is Socrates, Kattrin is St. Martin) but more important is that this is the "Song of Solomon" (from *Threepenny Opera*) and that Solomon is Courage herself:

> King Solomon was very wise
> So what's his history?
> He came to view this world with scorn
> Yes, he came to regret he ever had been born
> Declaring: all is vanity.
> King Solomon was very wise
> But long before the day was out
> The consequence was clear, alas:
> It was his wisdom brought him to this pass.
> A man is better off without.

I have heard the question asked whether this conclusion was not already reached in the "Song of the Great Capitulation" in Scene Four. Both songs are songs of defeat (Brecht's great subject) but of two different defeats. The second is defeat total and final: Courage has staked everything on wisdom, and wisdom has ruined her and her family. The first is the setback of "capitulation," that is of disenchantment. When Yvette was only seventeen she was in love, and love was heaven. Soon afterward she had learned to "fraternize behind the trees"; she had capitulated. It is perhaps hard to imagine Courage as a younger and different person from the woman we meet in the play, but in the "Song of the Great Capitulation" we are definitely invited to imagine her as a young woman who thought she could storm the heavens, whose faith seemed able to move mountains.

Scene Four is one of several in this play which one can regard as the whole play in miniature. For Brecht is not finished when he has set forth the character of Mother Courage as one who has passed from youthful idealism to cynical realism. For many a playwright, that would no doubt be that, but Courage's exchange with the angry young soldier leads to other things. We discover that Mother Courage is not a happy Machiavellian, boasting of her realism as an achievement. We find that she is deeply ashamed. And in finding this, we discover in Courage the mother of those two roaring idealists (not to say again: martyrs) Swiss Cheese and Kattrin. "Kiss my arse," says the soldier, and why? His bad language had not hitherto been directed at her. But she has been kind to him only to be cruel. If she has not broken his spirit, she has done something equally galling: she has made clear to him how easily his spirit can be broken. When you convert a person to the philosophy of You Can't Win, you can hardly expect to earn his gratitude at the same time.

In the way Courage puts matters to the soldier we see how close she came to being a truly wise woman. We also discover in this scene that, despite the confident tone of her cynical lingo, Courage is not really sure of herself and her little philosophy. She teaches the soldier that it is futile to protest, but she apparently does not know this herself until she reminds herself of it, for she has come here precisely to protest. Here we learn to recognize in Courage not only contradiction but conflict. She knows what she has thought. She is not sure what to think.

And this is communicated by Brecht in a very bold—or, if you prefer, just poetic—manner. For while Courage does not give herself to despair until the end (and not even then for those who can take at face value her: "I must get back into business"), she had correctly foreseen the end from the beginning: the despair she gives herself to had been there from the moment of capitulation. At times it would strike her between the eyes: she is very responsive and, for example, has worked out the Marxist interpretation of religion for herself. Scene Two contains a song she had taught Eilif as a boy: it accurately predicts the manner of his death. In Scene One she predicts doom for the whole family in her elaborate pantomime of fortune-telling. And it could be said that everything is there from the start, for the first thing Mother Courage does is to try and sell things by announcing an early death for her prospective customers. The famous "Song of Mother Courage" is the most extraordinary parody of the kind of song any real *vivandière* might try to attract customers with. Mother Courage's Come and buy! is nothing other than: Come and die! In that respect, her fortunetelling is on the level, and her wisdom is valid.

Scene Four, I have been saying, is one of several in this play which one can regard as the whole play in miniature. The main purpose of the play, for Brecht, was, I think, to generate anger over what it shows. Yet Brecht realizes how pointless angry plays have been—and angry speeches outside the drama. It is said that Clifford Odets' *Waiting for Lefty* made millionaires angry for as long as it took them to get from their seats to where their chauffeurs tactfully waited for them at the end of the block. Such is the anger of the social drama in general.

There is the anger of a sudden fit, which boils up and over and is gone. And there is the anger which informs the work of long years of change. *Why* can't the world be changed? For Mother Courage, it is not from any inherent unchangeability in the world. It is because our wish to change it is not strong enough. Nor is this weakness innate. It is simply that our objection to the present world isn't as strong as it once was. What is outrageous does not outrage us as it once did. Today, it only arouses the "short rage" of Brecht's soldier—and of Courage herself—not the long one that is required. Because we—they—have capitulated.

Capitulation is not just an idea but a feeling, an agony in fact, and is located not just in the scene of the Great Capitulation but in the whole play of *Mother Courage*.

Everything that happens is related to it, above all the things that are furthest away from it: namely, the deaths of Swiss Cheese and Kattrin. And if these children are what their mother made them, then their refusal to capitulate stems from her, is her own youth, her own original nature.

The ultimate achievement of an actress playing this role would be that she made us sense to what an extent Courage's children are truly hers.

—E.B.
1965

MOTHER COURAGE
AND HER CHILDREN

CHARACTERS

Mother Courage

Kattrin, *her dumb daughter*

Eilif, *her elder son*

Swiss Cheese, *her younger son*

Recruiting Officer

Sergeant

Cook

Swedish Commander

Chaplain

Ordnance Officer

Yvette Pottier

Man with the Bandage

Another Sergeant

Old Colonel

Clerk

Young Soldier

Older Soldier

Peasant

Peasant Woman

Young Man

Old Woman

Another Peasant

Another Peasant Woman

Young Peasant

Lieutenant

Voice

1

Spring, 1624. In Dalarna, the Swedish Commander Oxenstierna is recruiting for the campaign in Poland. The canteen woman Anna Fierling, commonly known as Mother Courage, loses a son.

Highway outside a town. A SERGEANT *and a* RECRUITING OFFICER *stand shivering.*

RECRUITING OFFICER: How the hell can you line up a squadron in a place like this? You know what I keep thinking about, Sergeant? Suicide. I'm supposed to knock four platoons together by the twelfth—four platoons the Chief's asking for! And they're so friendly around here, I'm scared to go to sleep at night. Suppose I do get my hands on some character and squint at him so I don't notice he's pigeon-chested and has varicose veins. I get him drunk and relaxed, he signs on the dotted line. I pay for the drinks, he steps outside for a minute. I have a hunch I should follow him to the door, and am I right? Off he's shot like a louse from a scratch. You can't take a man's word any more, Sergeant. There's no loyalty left in the world, no trust, no faith, no sense of honor. I'm losing my confidence in mankind, Sergeant.

SERGEANT: What they could use around here is a good war. What else can you expect with peace running wild all over the place? You know what the trouble with peace is? No organization. And when do you get organization? In a war. Peace is one big waste of equipment. Anything goes, no one gives a damn. See the way they eat? Cheese on pumpernickel, bacon on the cheese? Disgusting! How many horses have

23

they got in this town? How many young men? No-
body knows! They haven't bothered to count 'em!
That's peace for you! I've been in places where they
haven't had a war for seventy years and you know
what? The people haven't even been given names!
They don't know who they are! It takes a war to
fix that. In a war, everyone registers, everyone's
name's on a list. Their shoes are stacked, their corn's
in the bag, you count it all up—cattle, men, *et* cetera
—and you take it away! That's the story: no organization, no war!

RECRUITING OFFICER: It's the God's truth.

SERGEANT: Of course, a war's like any good deal: hard
to get going. But when it does get moving, it's a
pisser, and they're all scared of peace, like a dice
player who can't stop—'cause when peace comes they
have to pay up. Of course, *until* it gets going, they're
just as scared of war, it's such a novelty!

RECRUITING OFFICER: Hey, look, here's a canteen wagon.
Two women and a couple of fellows. Stop the old
lady, Sergeant. And if there's nothing doing this time,
you won't catch me freezing my ass in the April wind
any longer.

*A harmonica is heard. A canteen wagon rolls on,
drawn by two young fellows.* MOTHER COURAGE *is
sitting on it with her dumb daughter,* KATTRIN.

MOTHER COURAGE: A good day to you, Sergeant!

SERGEANT (*barring the way*): Good day to *you*! Who
d'you think *you* are?

MOTHER COURAGE: Tradespeople.

She sings:
Stop all the troops: here's Mother Courage!
Hey, Captain, let them come and buy!
For they can get from Mother Courage
Boots they will march in till they die!
Your marching men do not adore you

(Packs on their backs, lice in their hair)
But it's to death they're marching for you
And so they need good boots to wear!
  Christians, awake! Winter is gone!
  The snows depart! Dead men sleep on!
  Let all of you who still survive
  Get out of bed and look alive!

Your men will walk till they are dead, sir,
But cannot fight unless they eat.
The blood they spill for you is red, sir,
What fires that blood is my red meat.
Cannon is rough on empty bellies:
First with my meat they should be crammed.
Then let them go and find where hell is
And give my greetings to the damned!
  Christians, awake! Winter is gone!
  The snows depart! Dead men sleep on!
  Let all of you who still survive
  Get out of bed and look alive!

SERGEANT: Halt! Where are you from, riffraff?

EILIF: Second Finnish Regiment!

SERGEANT: Where are your papers?

MOTHER COURAGE: Papers?

SWISS CHEESE: But this is Mother Courage!

SERGEANT: Never heard of her. Where'd she get a name like that?

MOTHER COURAGE: They call me Mother Courage 'cause I was afraid I'd be ruined, so I drove through the bombardment of Riga like a madwoman, with fifty loaves of bread in my cart. They were going moldy, what else could I do?

SERGEANT: No funny business! Where are your papers?

MOTHER COURAGE (*rummaging among papers in a tin box and clambering down from her wagon*): Here, Sergeant! Here's a missal—I got it in Altötting to wrap my cucumbers in. Here's a map of Moravia— God khows if I'll ever get there—the birds can have

it if I don't. And here's a document saying my
horse hasn't got hoof and mouth disease—pity he
died on us, he cost fifteen guilders, thank God I
didn't pay it. Is that enough paper?

SERGEANT: Are you pulling my leg? Well, you've got
another guess coming. You need a license and you
know it.

MOTHER COURAGE: Show a little respect for a lady and
don't go telling these grown children of mine I'm
pulling anything of yours. What would I want with
you? My license in the Second Protestant Regiment
is an honest face. If *you* wouldn't know how to
read it, that's not my fault, I want no rubber stamp
on it anyhow.

RECRUITING OFFICER: Sergeant, we have a case of in-
subordination on our hands. Do you know what we
need in the army? Discipline!

MOTHER COURAGE: I was going to say sausages.

SERGEANT: Name?

MOTHER COURAGE: Anna Fierling.

SERGEANT: So you're all Fierlings.

MOTHER COURAGE: I was talking about me.

SERGEANT: And I was talking about your children.

MOTHER COURAGE: Must they all have the same name?
(*Pointing to the elder son:*) This fellow, for instance,
I call him Eilif Noyocki. Why? He got the name from
his father who told me he was called Koyocki. Or
was it Moyocki? Anyhow, the lad remembers him
to this day. Only the man he remembers is someone else, a Frenchman with a pointed beard. But
he certainly has his father's brains—that man could
whip the breeches off a farmer's backside before
he could turn around. So we all have our own
names.

SERGEANT: You're all called something different?

MOTHER COURAGE: Are you pretending you don't understand?

SERGEANT (*pointing at the younger son*): He's Chinese,
I suppose.

MOTHER COURAGE: Wrong again. Swiss.

SERGEANT: After the Frenchman?

MOTHER COURAGE: Frenchman? What Frenchman? Don't
confuse the issue, Sergeant, or we'll be here all day.
He's Swiss, but he happens to be called Feyos, a
name that has nothing to do with his father, who was
called something else—a military engineer, if you
please, and a drunkard.

SWISS CHEESE *nods, beaming; even* KATTRIN *smiles.*

SERGEANT: Then how come his name's Feyos?

MOTHER COURAGE: Oh, Sergeant, you have no imagina-
tion. *Of course* he's called Feyos: when he came,
I was with a Hungarian. He didn't mind. He had a
floating kidney, though he never touched a drop. He
was a vèry *honest* man. The boy takes after him.

SERGEANT: But that wasn't his father!

MOTHER COURAGE: I said: he took after him. I call him
Swiss Cheese. Why? Because he's good at pulling
wagons. (*Pointing to her daughter*:) And that is
Kattrin Haupt, she's half German.

SERGEANT: A nice family, I must say!

MOTHER COURAGE: And we've seen the whole wide world
together—this wagonload and me.

SERGEANT: We'll need all that in writing. (*He writes.*)
You're from Bamberg in Bavaria. What are you
doing *here?*

MOTHER COURAGE: I can't wait till the war is good enough
to come to Bamberg.

RECRUITING OFFICER: And you two oxen pull the cart.
Jacob Ox and Esau Ox! D'you ever get out of
harness?

EILIF: Mother! May I smack him in the puss? I'd like to.

MOTHER COURAGE: I'd like *you* to stay where you are.
And now, gentlemen, what about a brace of pistols?
Or a belt? Sergeant? Yours is worn clean through.

SERGEANT: It's something else *I'm* looking for. These lads of yours are straight as birch trees, strong limbs, massive chests. . . . What are such fine specimens doing out of the army?

MOTHER COURAGE (*quickly*): A soldier's life is not for sons of mine!

RECRUITING OFFICER: Why not? It means money. It means fame. Peddling shoes is woman's work. (*To* EILIF:) Step this way and let's see if that's muscle or chicken fat.

MOTHER COURAGE: It's chicken fat. Give him a good hard look, and he'll fall right over.

RECRUITING OFFICER: Yes, and kill a calf in the falling! (*He tries to hustle* EILIF *away*.)

MOTHER COURAGE: Let him alone! He's not for you!

RECRUITING OFFICER: He called my face a puss. That is an insult. The two of us will now go and settle the affair on the field of honor.

EILIF: Don't worry, Mother, I can handle him.

MOTHER COURAGE: Stay here. You're never happy till you're in a fight. He has a knife in his boot and he knows how to use it.

RECRUITING OFFICER: I'll draw it out of him like a milk tooth. Come on, young fellow!

MOTHER COURAGE: Officer, I'll report you to the Colonel, and he'll throw you in jail. His lieutenant is courting my daughter.

SERGEANT: Go easy. (*To* MOTHER COURAGE:) What have you got against the service, wasn't his own father a soldier? Didn't you say he died a soldier's death?

MOTHER COURAGE: This one's just a baby. You'll lead him like a lamb to the slaughter. I know you, you'll get five guilders for him.

RECRUITING OFFICER (*to* EILIF): First thing you know, you'll have a lovely cap and high boots, how about it?

EILIF: Not from you.

MOTHER COURAGE: "Let's you and me go fishing," said

the angler to the worm. (*To* SWISS CHEESE:) Run
and tell everybody they're trying to steal your
brother! (*She draws a knife.*) Yes, just you try, and
I'll cut you down like dogs! We sell cloth, we sell
ham, we are peaceful people!

SERGEANT: You're peaceful all right: your knife proves
that. Why, you should be ashamed of yourself. Give
me that knife, you hag! You admit you live off the
war, what else *could* you live off? Now tell me, how
can we have a war without soldiers?

MOTHER COURAGE: Do they have to be mine?

SERGEANT: So that's the trouble. The war should swallow
the peach stone and spit out the peach, hm? Your
brood should get fat off the war, but the poor war
must ask nothing in return, it can look after itself,
can it? Call yourself Mother Courage and then
get scared of the war, your breadwinner? Your sons
aren't scared, I know that much.

EILIF: Takes more than a war to scare me.

SERGEANT: Correct! Take me. The soldier's life hasn't
done *me* any harm, has it? I enlisted at seventeen.

MOTHER COURAGE: You haven't reached seventy.

SERGEANT: I will, though.

MOTHER COURAGE: Above ground?

SERGEANT: Are you trying to rile me, telling me I'll die?

MOTHER COURAGE: Suppose it's the truth? Suppose I see
it's your fate? Suppose I *know* you're just a corpse
on furlough?

SWISS CHEESE: She can look into the future. Everyone
says so.

RECRUITING OFFICER: Then by all means look into the
sergeant's future. It might amuse him.

SERGEANT: I don't believe in that stuff.

MOTHER COURAGE: Helmet!

The SERGEANT *gives her his helmet.*

SERGEANT: It means less than a crap in the grass. Anything for a laugh.

MOTHER COURAGE (*taking a sheet of parchment and tearing it in two*): Eilif, Swiss Cheese, Kattrin! So shall we all be torn in two if we let ourselves get too deep into this war! (*To the* SERGEANT:) I'll give you the bargain rate, and do it free. Watch! Death is black, so I draw a black cross.

SWISS CHEESE: And the other she leaves blank, see?

MOTHER COURAGE: I fold them, put them in the helmet, and mix 'em up together, the way we're all mixed up together from our mother's womb on. Now draw!

The SERGEANT *hesitates.*

RECRUITING OFFICER (*to* EILIF): I don't take just anybody. I'm choosy. And you've got guts, I like that.

SERGEANT (*fishing around in the helmet*): It's silly. Means as much as blowing your nose.

SWISS CHEESE: The black cross! Oh, his number's up!

RECRUITING OFFICER: Don't let them get under your skin. There aren't enough bullets to go around.

SERGEANT (*hoarsely*): You cheated me!

MOTHER COURAGE: You cheated yourself the day you enlisted. And now we must drive on. There isn't a war every day in the week, we must get to work.

SERGEANT: Hell, you're not getting away with this! We're taking that bastard of yours with *us*!

EILIF: I'd like that, Mother.

MOTHER COURAGE: Quiet—you Finnish devil, you!

EILIF: And Swiss Cheese wants to be a soldier, too.

MOTHER COURAGE: That's news to me. I see I'll have to draw lots for all three of you. (*She goes to the back to draw the crosses on bits of paper.*)

RECRUITING OFFICER (*to* EILIF): People've been saying the Swedish soldier is religious. That kind of loose talk has hurt us a lot. One verse of a hymn every Sunday—and then only if you have a voice . . .

MOTHER COURAGE (*returning with the slips and putting them in the* SERGEANT's *helmet*): So they'd desert their old mother, would they, the scoundrels? They take to war like a cat to cream. But I'll consult these slips, and they'll see the world's no promised land, with a "Join up, son, you're officer material!" Sergeant, I'm afraid for them, very afraid they won't get through this war. They have terrible qualities, all three. (*She holds the helmet out to* EILIF.) There. Draw your lot. (EILIF *fishes in the helmet, unfolds a slip. She snatches it from him.*) There you have it: a cross. Unhappy mother that I am, rich only in a mother's sorrows! He dies. In the springtime of his life, he must go. If he's a soldier, he must bite the dust, that's clear. He's too brave, like his father. And if he doesn't use his head, he'll go the way of all flesh, the slip proves it. (*Hectoring him:*) Will you use your head?

EILIF: Why not?

MOTHER COURAGE: It's using your head to stay with your mother. And when they make fun of you and call you a chicken, just laugh.

RECRUITING OFFICER: If you're going to wet your pants, I'll try your brother.

MOTHER COURAGE: I told you to laugh. Laugh! Now it's your turn, Swiss Cheese. You should be a better bet, you're honest. (*He fishes in the helmet.*) Why are you giving that slip such a funny look? You've drawn a blank for sure. It can't be there's a cross on it. It can't be I'm going to lose *you*. (*She takes the slip.*) A cross? Him too! Could it be 'cause he's so simple? Oh, Swiss Cheese, you'll be a goner too, if you aren't honest, honest, honest the whole time, the way I always brought you up to be, the way you always bring me all the change when you buy me a loaf. It's the only way you can save yourself. Look, Sergeant, if it isn't a black cross!

SERGEANT: It's a cross! I don't understand how *I* got one. I always stay well in the rear. (*To the* OFFICER:) But it can't be a trick: it gets *her* children too.

SWISS CHEESE: It gets me too. But I don't accept it!

MOTHER COURAGE (*to* KATTRIN): And now all I have left for certain is you, you're a cross in yourself, you have a good heart. (*She holds the helmet up high toward the wagon but takes the slip out herself.*) Oh, I could give up in despair! There must be some mistake, I didn't mix them right. Don't be too kind, Kattrin, just don't, there's a cross in your path too. Always be very quiet, it can't be hard, you can't speak. Well, so now you know, all of you: be careful, you'll need to be. Now let's climb on the wagon and move on. (*She returns the helmet to the* SERGEANT *and climbs on the wagon.*)

RECRUITING OFFICER (*to the* SERGEANT): Do something!

SERGEANT: I don't feel very well.

RECRUITING OFFICER: Maybe you caught a chill when you handed over your helmet in this wind. Get her involved in a business transaction! (*Aloud.*) That belt, Sergeant, you could at least take a look at it. These good people live by trade, don't they? Hey, all of you, the sergeant wants to buy the belt!

MOTHER COURAGE: Half a guilder. A belt like that is worth two guilders. (*She clambers down again from the wagon.*)

SERGEANT: It isn't new. But there's too much wind here. I'll go and look at it behind the wagon. (*He does so.*)

MOTHER COURAGE: I don't find it windy.

SERGEANT: Maybe it's worth half a guilder at that. There's silver on it.

MOTHER COURAGE (*following him behind the wagon*): A solid six ounces worth!

RECRUITING OFFICER (*to* EILIF): And we can have a drink, just us men. I'll advance you some money to cover it. Let's go.

EILIF *stands undecided.*

MOTHER COURAGE: Half a guilder, then.

SERGEANT: I don't understand it. I always stay in the rear. There's no safer spot for a sergeant to be. You

can send the others on ahead in quest of fame. My
appetite is ruined. I can tell you right now: I won't
be able to get anything down.

MOTHER COURAGE: You shouldn't take on so, just because
you can't eat. Just stay in the rear. Here, take a
slug of brandy, man. (*She gives him brandy.*)

RECRUITING OFFICER (*taking* EILIF *by the arm and making off toward the back*): Ten guilders in advance
and you're a soldier of the king and a stout fellow
and the women will be mad about you. And you
can give me a smack in the puss for insulting you.

Both leave.
Dumb KATTRIN *jumps down from the wagon and
lets out harsh cries.*

MOTHER COURAGE: Coming, Kattrin, coming! The sergeant's just paying up. (*She bites the half guilder.*)
I'm suspicious of all money, I've been badly burned,
Sergeant. But this money's good. And now we'll be
going. Where's Eilif?

SWISS CHEESE: Gone with the recruiting officer.

MOTHER COURAGE (*standing quite still, then*): Oh, you
simpleton! (*To* KATTRIN:) You *can't* speak, I know.
You are innocent.

SERGEANT: That's life. Take a slug yourself, Mother.
Being a soldier isn't the worst that could happen.
You want to live off war and keep you and yours
out of it, do you?

MOTHER COURAGE: You must help your brother now,
Kattrin.

*Brother and sister get into harness together and pull
the wagon.* MOTHER COURAGE *walks at their side.
The wagon gets under way.*

SERGEANT (*looking after them*):
When a war gives you all you earn
One day it may claim something in return!

2

In the years 1625 and 1626 Mother Courage journeys through Poland in the baggage train of the Swedish army. She meets her son again before the fortified town of Wallhof.—Of the successful sale of a capon and great days for the brave son.

Tent of the SWEDISH COMMANDER. *Kitchen next to it. Thunder of cannon. The* COOK *is quarreling with* MOTHER COURAGE, *who is trying to sell him a capon.*

COOK: Sixty hellers for that miserable bird?

MOTHER COURAGE: Miserable bird? This fat fowl? Your Commander is a glutton. Woe betide you if you've nothing for him to eat. This capon is worth sixty hellers to you.

COOK: They're ten hellers a dozen on every corner.

MOTHER COURAGE: A capon like this on every corner! With a siege going on and people all skin and bones? Maybe you can get a field rat! I said maybe. Because we're all out of *them* too. Don't you see the soldiers running five deep after one hungry little field rat? All right then, in a siege, my price for a giant capon is fifty hellers.

COOK: But we're not "in a siege," we're doing the besieging, it's the other side that's "in a siege," when will you get this into your head?

MOTHER COURAGE: A fat lot of difference that makes, *we* haven't got a thing to eat either. They took everything into the town with them before all this started, and now they've nothing to do but eat and drink, I hear. It's us I'm worried about. Look at the farmers around here, they haven't a thing.

34

COOK: Certainly they have. They hide it.

MOTHER COURAGE (*triumphant*): They have not! They're ruined, that's what. They're so hungry I've seen 'em digging up roots to eat. I could boil your leather belt and make their mouths water with it. That's how things are around here. And I'm expected to let a capon go for forty hellers!

COOK: Thirty. Not forty. I said thirty hellers.

MOTHER COURAGE: I say this is no ordinary capon. It was a talented animal, so I hear. It would only feed to music—one march in particular was its favorite. It was so intelligent it could count. Forty hellers is too much for all this? I know *your* problem: if you don't find something to eat and quick, the Chief will—cut—your—fat—head—off!

COOK: All right, just watch. (*He takes a piece of beef and lays his knife on it.*) Here's a piece of beef, I'm going to roast it. I give you one more chance.

MOTHER COURAGE: Roast it, go ahead, it's only one year old.

COOK: One *day* old! Yesterday it was a cow. I saw it running around.

MOTHER COURAGE: In that case it must have started stinking before it died.

COOK: I don't care if I have to cook it for five hours. We'll see if it's still hard after that. (*He cuts into it.*)

MOTHER COURAGE: Put plenty of pepper in, so the Commander won't smell the smell.

The SWEDISH COMMANDER, *a* CHAPLAIN, *and* EILIF *enter the tent.*

COMMANDER (*clapping* EILIF *on the shoulder*): In the Commander's tent with you, my son! Sit at my right hand, you happy warrior! You've played a hero's part, you've served the Lord in his own Holy War, *that's* the thing! And you'll get a gold bracelet out of it when we take the town if *I* have any say in the matter! We come to save their souls and what do they do, the filthy, shameless peasant pigs? Drive their cattle away from *us*, while they stuff their priests with beef at both ends! But you showed 'em. So here's a can of red wine for you, we'll drink together! (*They do so.*) The chaplain gets the dregs, he's pious. Now what would you like for dinner, my hearty?

EILIF: How about a slice of meat?

COMMANDER: Cook, meat!

COOK: Nothing to eat, so he brings company to eat it!

MOTHER COURAGE *makes him stop talking; she wants to listen.*

EILIF: Tires you out, skinning peasants. Gives you an appetite.

MOTHER COURAGE: Dear God, it's my Eilif!

COOK: Who?

MOTHER COURAGE: My eldest. It's two years since I saw him, he was stolen from me in the street. He must be in high favor if the Commander's invited him to dinner. And what do you have to eat? Nothing. You hear what the Commander's guest wants? Meat! Better take my advice, buy the capon. The price is one guilder.

The COMMANDER *has sat down with* EILIF *and the* CHAPLAIN.

COMMANDER (*roaring*): Cook! Dinner, you pig, or I'll have your head!

COOK: This is blackmail. Give me the damn thing!

MOTHER COURAGE: A miserable bird like this?

COOK: You were right. Give it here. It's highway robbery, fifty hellers.

MOTHER COURAGE: I said one guilder. Nothing's too high for my eldest, the Commander's guest of honor.

COOK (*giving her the money*): Well, you might at least pluck it till I have a fire going.

MOTHER COURAGE (*sitting down to pluck the capon*): I can't wait to see his face when he sees me. This is my brave and clever son. I have a stupid one as well but he's honest. The daughter is nothing. At least, she doesn't talk: we must be thankful for small mercies.

COMMANDER: Have another can, my son, it's my favorite Falernian. There's only one cask left—two at the most—but it's worth it to meet a soldier that still believes in God! The shepherd of our flock here just looks on, he only preaches, he hasn't a clue how anything gets done. So now, Eilif, my son, give us the details: tell us how you fixed the peasants and grabbed the twenty bullocks. And let's hope they'll soon be here.

EILIF: In one day's time. Two at the most.

MOTHER COURAGE: Now that's considerate of Eilif—to bring the oxen tomorrow—otherwise my capon wouldn't have been so welcome today.

EILIF: Well, it was like this. I found out that the peasants had hidden their oxen and—on the sly and chiefly at night—had driven them into a certain wood. The people from the town were to pick them up there. I let them get their oxen in peace—they ought to know better than me where they are, I said to myself. Meanwhile I made my men crazy for meat. Their rations were short and I made sure they got shorter. Their mouths'd water at the sound of any word beginning with MEA . . . , like measles.

COMMANDER: Smart fella.

EILIF: Not bad. The rest was a snap. Only the peasants had clubs and outnumbered us three to one and made a murderous attack on us. Four of them drove me into a clump of trees, knocked my good sword from my hand, and yelled, "Surrender!" What now, I said to myself, they'll make mincemeat of me.

COMMANDER: What did you do?

EILIF: I laughed.

COMMANDER: You what?

EILIF: I laughed. And so we got to talking. I came right down to business and said: "Twenty guilders an ox is too much, I bid fifteen." Like I wanted to buy. That foxed 'em. So while they were scratching their heads, I reached for my good sword and cut 'em to pieces. Necessity knows no law, huh?

COMMANDER: What do *you* say, shepherd of the flock?

CHAPLAIN: Strictly speaking, that saying is not in the Bible. Our Lord made five hundred loaves out of five so that no such necessity would arise. When he told men to love their neighbors, their bellies were full. Things have changed since his day.

COMMANDER (*laughing*): Things have changed! A swallow of wine for those wise words, you pharisee! (*To* EILIF:) You cut 'em to pieces in a good cause, our fellows were hungry and you gave 'em to eat. Doesn't it say in the Bible "Whatsoever thou doest for the least of these my children, thou doest for me?" And what *did* you do for 'em? You got 'em the best steak dinner they ever tasted. Moldy bread is not what they're used to. They always ate white bread, and drank wine in their helmets, before going out to fight for God.

EILIF: I reached for my good sword and cut 'em to pieces.

COMMANDER: You have the makings of a Julius Caesar, why, you should be presented to the King!

EILIF: I've seen him—from a distance of course. He seemed to shed a light all around. I must try to be like him!

COMMANDER: I think you're succeeding, my boy! Oh, Eilif, you don't know how I value a brave soldier like you! I treat such a chap as my very own son. (*He takes him to the map.*) Take a look at our position, Eilif, it isn't all it might be, is it?

MOTHER COURAGE *has been listening and is now plucking angrily at her capon.*

MOTHER COURAGE: He must be a very bad Commander.

COOK: Just a gluttonous one. Why bad?

MOTHER COURAGE: Because he needs *brave* soldiers, that's why. If his plan of campaign was any good, why would he need *brave* soldiers, wouldn't plain, ordinary soldiers do? Whenever there are great virtues, it's a sure sign something's wrong.

COOK: You mean, it's a sure sign something's right.

MOTHER COURAGE: I mean what I say. Why? When a general or a king is stupid and leads his soldiers into a trap, they need this virtue of courage. When he's tightfisted and hasn't enough soldiers, the few he does have need the heroism of Hercules—another virtue. And if he's slovenly and doesn't give a damn about anything, they have to be as wise as serpents or they're finished. Loyalty's another virtue and you need plenty of it if the king's always asking too much of you. All virtues which a well-regulated country with a good king or a good general wouldn't need. In a good country virtues wouldn't be necessary. Everybody could be quite ordinary, middling, and, for all I care, cowards.

COMMANDER: I bet your father was a soldier.

EILIF: I've heard he was a great soldier. My mother warned me. I know a song about that.

COMMANDER: Sing it to us. (*Roaring:*) Bring that meat!

EILIF: It's called The Song of the Wise Woman and the Soldier.

He sings and at the same time does a war dance with his saber:

A shotgun will shoot and a jackknife will knife,
If you wade in the water, it will drown you,
Keep away from the ice, if you want my advice,
Said the wise woman to the soldier.

But that young soldier, he loaded his gun,
And he reached for his knife, and he started to run:

For marching never could hurt him!
From the north to the south he will march through
the land
With his knife at his side and his gun in his hand:
That's what the soldiers told the wise woman.

Woe to him who defies the advice of the wise!
If you wade in the water, it will drown you!
Don't ignore what I say or you'll rue it one day,
Said the wise woman to the soldier.

But that young soldier, his knife at his side
And his gun in his hand, he steps into the tide:
For water never could hurt him!
When the new moon is shining on yonder church
tower
We are all coming back: go and pray for that hour:
That's what the soldiers told the wise woman.

MOTHER COURAGE (*continues the song from her kitchen,
beating on a pan with a spoon*):

Then the wise woman spoke: you will vanish like
smoke
Leaving nothing but cold air behind you!
Just watch the smoke fly! Oh God, don't let him
die!
Said the wise woman to the soldier.

EILIF: What's that?

MOTHER COURAGE (*singing on*):

And the lad who defied the wise woman's advice,
When the new moon shone, floated down with the ice:
He waded in the water and it drowned him.

The wise woman spoke, and they vanished like smoke,
And their glorious deeds did not warm us.
Your glorious deeds do not warm us!

COMMANDER: What a kitchen I've got! There's no end
to the liberties they take!

EILIF *has entered the kitchen and embraced his mother.*

EILIF: To see you again! Where are the others?

MOTHER COURAGE (*in his arms*): Happy as ducks in a pond. Swiss Cheese is paymaster with the Second Regiment, so at least he isn't in the fighting. I couldn't keep him out altogether.

EILIF: Are your feet holding up?

MOTHER COURAGE: I've a bit of trouble getting my shoes on in the morning.

The COMMANDER *has come over.*

COMMANDER: So you're his mother! I hope you have more sons for me like this fellow.

EILIF: If I'm not the lucky one: to be feasted by the Commander while you sit listening in the kitchen!

MOTHER COURAGE: Yes. I heard all right. (*She gives him a box on the ear.*)

EILIF (*his hand on his cheek*): Because I took the oxen?

MOTHER COURAGE: No. Because you didn't surrender when the four peasants let fly at you and tried to make mincemeat of you! Didn't I teach you to take care of yourself? You Finnish devil, you!

The COMMANDER *and the* CHAPLAIN *stand laughing in the doorway.*

3

Three years pass and Mother Courage, with parts of a Finnish regiment, is taken prisoner. Her daughter is saved, her wagon likewise, but her honest son dies.

A camp. The regimental flag is flying from a pole. Afternoon. All sorts of wares hanging on the wagon. MOTHER COURAGE's *clothesline is tied to the wagon at one end, to a cannon at the other. She and* KATTRIN *are folding the washing on the cannon. At the same time she is bargaining with an* ORDNANCE OFFICER *over a bag of bullets.* SWISS CHEESE, *in paymaster's uniform now, looks on.* YVETTE POTTIER, *a very good-looking young person, is sewing at a colored hat, a glass of brandy before her. She is in stocking feet. Her red boots are near by.*

OFFICER: I'm letting you have the bullets for two guilders. Dirt cheap. 'Cause I need the money. The Colonel's been drinking with the officers for three days and we're out of liquor.

MOTHER COURAGE: They're army property. If they find 'em on me, I'll be court-martialed. You sell your bullets, you bastards, and send your men out to fight with nothing to shoot with.

OFFICER: Oh, come on, you scratch my back, and I'll scratch yours.

MOTHER COURAGE: I won't take army stuff. Not at *that* price.

OFFICER: You can resell 'em for five guilders, maybe eight, to the Ordnance Officer of the Fourth Regiment. All you have to do is give him a receipt for twelve. He hasn't a bullet left.

MOTHER COURAGE: Why don't you do it yourself?

OFFICER: I don't trust him. We're friends.

MOTHER COURAGE (*taking the bag*): Give it here. (*To* KATTRIN:) Take it around to the back and pay him a guilder and a half. (*As the* OFFICER *protests*:) I said a guilder and a half! (KATTRIN *drags the bag away. The* OFFICER *follows.* MOTHER COURAGE *speaks to* SWISS CHEESE:) Here's your underwear back, take care of it; it's October now, autumn may come at any time; I purposely don't say it must come, I've learned from experience there's nothing that must come, not even the seasons. But your books *must* balance now you're the regimental paymaster. *Do* they balance?

SWISS CHEESE: Yes, Mother.

MOTHER COURAGE: Don't forget they made you paymaster because you're honest and so simple you'd never think of running off with the cash. Don't lose that underwear.

SWISS CHEESE: No, mother. I'll put it under the mattress. (*He starts to go.*)

OFFICER: I'll go with you, paymaster.

MOTHER COURAGE: Don't teach him any monkey business.

Without a good-by the OFFICER *leaves with* SWISS CHEESE.

YVETTE (*waving to him*): You might at least say good-by!

MOTHER COURAGE (*to* YVETTE): I don't like that. *He's* no sort of company for my Swiss Cheese. But the war's not making a bad start. Before all the different countries get into it, four or five years'll have gone by like nothing. If I look ahead and make no mistakes, business will be good. Don't you know you shouldn't drink in the morning with your illness?

YVETTE: Who says I'm ill? That's libel!

MOTHER COURAGE: They all say so.

YVETTE: They're all liars. I'm desperate, Mother Courage.

They all avoid me like a stinking fish. Because of those lies. So what am I arranging my hat for? (*She throws it down.*) That's why I drink in the morning. I never used to, it gives you crow's feet. But what's the difference? Every man in the regiment knows me. I should have stayed at home when my first was unfaithful. But pride isn't for the likes of us, you eat dirt or down you go.

MOTHER COURAGE: Now don't you start again with your friend Peter and how it all happened—in front of my innocent daughter.

YVETTE: She's the one that should hear it. So she'll get hardened against love.

MOTHER COURAGE: That's something no one ever gets hardened against.

YVETTE: I'll tell you about it, and get it off my chest. I grew up in Flanders' fields, that's where it starts, or I'd never even have caught sight of him and I wouldn't be here in Poland today. He was an army cook, blond, a Dutchman, but thin. Kattrin, beware of thin men! I didn't. I didn't even know he'd had another girl before me and she called him Peter Piper because he never took his pipe out of his mouth the whole time, it meant so little to him.

She sings "The Fraternization Song":

> When I was almost seventeen
> The foe came to our land
> And laying aside his saber
> He took me gently by the hand.

> First came the May Day Rite
> Then came the May Day night.
> The pipes played and the drums did beat.
> The foe paraded down the street.
> And then with us they took their ease
> And fraternized behind the trees.

> Our foes they came in plenty.

A cook was my own foe.
I hated him by daylight
But in the dark I loved him so.

> First comes the May Day Rite
> Then comes the May Day night.
> The pipes play and the drums do beat.
> The foe parades down every street.
> And then with us they take their ease
> And fraternize behind the trees.

The heavens seemed to open
Such passion did I feel.
But my people never understood
The love I felt was real.

> One day the sun rose slow
> On all my pain and woe.
> My loved one, with the other men,
> Presented arms and stood at ease
> Then marched away past all those trees
> And never did come back again.

I made the mistake of running after him, I never
found him. It's five years ago now. (*With swaying
gait she goes behind the wagon.*)

MOTHER COURAGE: You've left your hat.
YVETTE: For the birds.
MOTHER COURAGE: Let this be a lesson to you, Kattrin,
never start anything with a soldier. The heavens
do seem to open, so watch out! Even with men who're
not in the army life's no honeypot. He tells you
he'd like to kiss the ground under your feet—did
you wash 'em yesterday, while we're on the subject?—and then if you don't look out, your number's
up, you're his slave for life. Be glad you're dumb,
Kattrin: you'll never contradict yourself, you'll never
want to bite your tongue off because you spoke
out of turn. Dumbness is a gift from God. Here

comes the Commander's cook, what's bothering *him*?

Enter the COOK *and the* CHAPLAIN.

CHAPLAIN: I bring a message from your son Eilif. The cook came with me. You've made, ahem, an impression on him.

COOK: I thought I'd get a little whiff of the balmy breeze.

MOTHER COURAGE: You're welcome to that if you behave yourself, and even if you don't I think I can handle you. But what does Eilif want? I don't have any money.

CHAPLAIN: Actually, I have something to tell his brother, the paymaster.

MOTHER COURAGE: He isn't here. And he isn't anywhere else either. He's not his brother's paymaster, and I won't have him led into temptation. Let Eilif try it on with someone else! (*She takes money from the purse at her belt.*) Give him this. It's a sin. He's speculating in mother love, he ought to be ashamed of himself.

COOK: Not for long. He has to go with his regiment now —to his death maybe. Send some more money, or you'll be sorry. You women are hard—and sorry afterward. A glass of brandy wouldn't cost very much, but you refuse to provide it, and six feet under goes your man and you can't dig him up again.

CHAPLAIN: All very touching, my dear cook, but to fall in this war is not a misfortune, it's a blessing. This is a war of religion. Not just any old war but a special one, a religious one, and therefore pleasing unto God.

COOK: Correct. In one sense it's a war because there's fleecing, bribing, plundering, not to mention a little raping, but it's different from all other wars because it's a war of religion. That's clear. All the same, it makes you thirsty.

CHAPLAIN (*to* MOTHER COURAGE, *pointing at the* COOK): I

tried to hold him off but he said you'd bewitched him. He dreams about you.

COOK (*lighting a clay pipe*): Brandy from the fair hand of a lady, that's for me. And don't embarrass me any more: the stories the chaplain was telling me on the way over still have me blushing.

MOTHER COURAGE: A man of his cloth! I must get you both something to drink or you'll be making improper advances out of sheer boredom.

CHAPLAIN: That is indeed a temptation, said the court chaplain, and gave way to it. (*Turning toward KATTRIN as he walks:*) And who is this captivating young person?

MOTHER COURAGE: She's not a captivating young person, she a respectable young person.

The CHAPLAIN *and the* COOK *go with* MOTHER COURAGE *behind the cart, and one hears them talk politics.*

MOTHER COURAGE: The trouble here in Poland is that the Poles *would* keep meddling. It's true our King moved in on them with man, beast, and wagon, but instead of keeping the peace the Poles attacked the Swedish King when he was in the act of peacefully withdrawing. So they were guilty of a breach of the peace and their blood is on their own heads.

CHAPLAIN: Anyway, our King was thinking of nothing but freedom. The Kaiser enslaved them all, Poles and Germans alike, so our King *had* to liberate them.

COOK: Just what *I* think. Your health! Your brandy is first-rate, I'm never mistaken in a face.

KATTRIN *looks after them, leaves the washing, goes to the hat, picks it up, sits down, and takes up the red boots.*

And the war is a war of religion. (*Singing while* KATTRIN *puts the boots on:*) "A mighty fortress is our God . . ." (*He sings a verse or so of Luther's hymn.*) And talking of King Gustavus, this freedom he tried to bring to Germany cost him a pretty penny. Back in Sweden he had to levy a salt tax, the poorer folks didn't like it a bit. Then, too, he had to lock up the Germans and even cut their heads off, they clung so to slavery and their Kaiser. Of course, if no one had *wanted* to be free, the King would have got quite mad. First it was just Poland he tried to protect from bad men, especially the Kaiser, then his appetite grew with eating, and he ended up protecting Germany too. Now Germany put up a pretty decent fight. So the good King had nothing but worries in return for his outlay and his goodness, and of course he had to get his money back with taxes, which made bad blood, but he didn't shrink even from that. For he had one thing in his favor anyway, God's Holy Word, which was all to the good, because otherwise they could have said he did it for profit. That's how he kept his conscience clear. He always put conscience first.

MOTHER COURAGE: It's plain you're no Swede, or you'd speak differently of the Hero King.

CHAPLAIN: What's more, you eat his bread.

COOK: I don't eat his bread. I bake his bread.

MOTHER COURAGE: He's unbeatable. Why? His men believe in him. (*Earnestly:*) To hear the big fellows talk, they wage war from fear of God and for all things bright and beautiful, but just look into it, and you'll see they're not so silly: they want a good profit out of it, or else the little fellows like you and me wouldn't back 'em up.

COOK: That's right.

CHAPLAIN: And as a Dutchman you'd do well to see which flag's flying here before you express an opinion!

MOTHER COURAGE: All good Protestants forever!

COOK: A health!

KATTRIN *has begun to strut about with* YVETTE'S

hat on, copying YVETTE'S *sexy walk. Suddenly cannon and shots. Drums.* MOTHER COURAGE, *the* COOK, *and the* CHAPLAIN *rush around to the front of the cart, the last two with glasses in their hands. The* ORDNANCE OFFICER *and a* SOLDIER *come running to the cannon and try to push it along.*

MOTHER COURAGE: What's the matter? Let me get my washing off that gun, you slobs! (*She tries to do so.*)

OFFICER: The Catholics! Surprise attack! We don't know if we can get away! (*To the* SOLDIER:) Get that gun! (*He runs off.*)

COOK: For heaven's sake! I must go to the Commander. Mother Courage, I'll be back in a day or two—for a short conversation. (*He rushes off.*)

MOTHER COURAGE: Hey, you've left your pipe!

COOK (*off*): Keep it for me, I'll need it!

MOTHER COURAGE: This *would* happen just when we were making money.

CHAPLAIN: Well, I must be going too. Yes, if the enemy's so close, it can be dangerous. "Blessed are the peacemakers," a good slogan in war time! If only I had a cloak.

MOTHER COURAGE: I'm lending no cloaks. Not even to save a life, I'm not. I've had experience in that line.

CHAPLAIN: But I'm in special danger. Because of my religion.

MOTHER COURAGE (*bringing him a cloak*): It's against my better judgment. Now run!

CHAPLAIN: I thank you, you're very generous, but maybe I'd better stay and sit here. If I run, I might attract the enemy's attention, I might arouse suspicion.

MOTHER COURAGE (*to the* SOLDIER): Let it alone, you dolt, who's going to pay you for this? It'll cost you your life, let me hold it for you.

SOLDIER (*running away*): You're my witness: I tried!

MOTHER COURAGE: I'll swear to it! (*Seeing* KATTRIN *with the hat:*) What on earth are you up to—with a whore's hat! Take it off this minute! Are you mad? With the enemy coming? (*She tears the hat off her head.*) Do you want them to find you and make a whore of you? And she has the boots on too, straight from Babylon. I'll soon fix that. (*She tries to get them off.*) Oh, God, Chaplain, help me with these boots, I'll be right back. (*She runs to the wagon.*)

YVETTE (*entering and powdering her face*): What's that you say: the Catholics are coming? Where's my hat? Who's been trampling on it? I can't run around in that, what will they think of me? And I don't even have a mirror. (*To the* CHAPLAIN:) How do I look —too much powder?

CHAPLAIN: Just, er, right.

YVETTE: And where are my red boots? (*She can't find them because* KATTRIN *is hiding her feet under her skirt.*) I left them here! Now I've got to go barefoot to my tent, it's a scandal! (*Exit.*)

SWISS CHEESE *comes running in carrying a cash box.* MOTHER COURAGE *enters with her hands covered with ashes.*

MOTHER COURAGE (*to* KATTRIN): Ashes! (*To* SWISS CHEESE:) What have you got there?

SWISS CHEESE: The regimental cash box.

MOTHER COURAGE: Throw it away! Your paymastering days are over!

SWISS CHEESE: It's a trust! (*He goes to the back.*)

MOTHER COURAGE (*to the* CHAPLAIN): Off with your pastor's cloak, Chaplain, or they'll recognize you, cloak or no cloak. (*She is rubbing ashes into* KATTRIN'*s face.*) Keep still. A little dirt, and you're safe. A calamity! The sentries were drunk. Well, one must hide one's light under a bushel, as they say. When a soldier sees a clean face, there's one more whore in the world. Especially a Catholic soldier. For weeks on end, no grub. Then, when the plundering starts and they steal some, they jump on top of the women-

folk. That should do. Let me look at you. Not bad.
Looks like you've been rolling in muck. Don't trem-
ble. Nothing can happen to you now. (*To* SWISS
CHEESE:) Where've you left the cash box?

SWISS CHEESE: I thought I'd just put it in the wagon.

MOTHER COURAGE (*horrified*): What! In my wagon? God
punish you for a prize idiot! If I just look away for a
moment! They'll hang all three of us!

SWISS CHEESE: Then I'll put it somewhere else. Or escape
with it.

MOTHER COURAGE: You'll stay where you are. It's too late.

CHAPLAIN (*still changing his clothes*): For heaven's sake:
the flag!

MOTHER COURAGE (*taking down the flag*): God in heaven!
I don't notice it any more. I've had it twenty-five
years.

The thunder of cannon grows.

Three days later. Morning. The cannon is gone.
MOTHER COURAGE, KATTRIN, *the* CHAPLAIN, *and*
SWISS CHEESE *sit anxiously eating.*

SWISS CHEESE: This is the third day I've been sitting here
doing nothing, and the Sergeant, who's always been
patient with me, may be slowly beginning to ask,
"Where on earth is Swiss Cheese with that cash box?"

MOTHER COURAGE: Be glad they're not on the trail.

CHAPLAIN: What about me? I can't hold a service here or
I'll be in hot water. It is written, "Out of the abun-
dance of the heart, the tongue speaketh." But woe
is me if *my* tongue speaketh!

MOTHER COURAGE: That's how it is. Here you sit—one
with his religion, the other with his cash box, I don't
know which is more dangerous.

CHAPLAIN: We're in God's hands now!

MOTHER COURAGE: I hope we're not *that* desperate, but it
is hard to sleep nights. 'Course it'd be easier if *you*
weren't here, Swiss Cheese, all the same I've not done
badly. I told them I was against the Antichrist, who's

a Swede with horns on his head. I told them I noticed
his left horn's a bit threadbare. When they cross-
examined me, I always asked where I could buy holy
candles a bit cheaper. I know these things because
Swiss Cheese's father was a Catholic and made jokes
about it. They didn't quite believe me but they needed
a canteen, so they turned a blind eye. Maybe it's all
for the best. We're prisoners. But so are lice in fur.

CHAPLAIN: The milk is good. As far as quantity goes, we
may have to reduce our Swedish appetites somewhat.
We are defeated.

MOTHER COURAGE: Who's defeated? The defeats and victories of the fellows at the top aren't always defeats
and victories for the fellows at the bottom. Not at all.
There've been cases where a defeat is a victory for
the fellows at the bottom, it's only their honor that's
lost, nothing serious. In Livonia once, our Chief took
such a knock from the enemy, in the confusion I got
a fine gray mare out of the baggage train, it pulled
my wagon seven months—till we won and there was
an inventory. But in general both defeat and victory
are a costly business for us that haven't got much.
The best thing is for politics to get stuck in the
mud. (*To* SWISS CHEESE:) Eat!

SWISS CHEESE: I don't like it. How will the sergeant pay
his men?

MOTHER COURAGE: Soldiers in flight don't get paid.

SWISS CHEESE: Well, they could claim to be. No pay, no
flight. They can refuse to budge.

MOTHER COURAGE: Swiss Cheese, your sense of duty
worries me. I've brought you up to be honest because you're not very bright. But don't overdo it.
And now I'm going with the chaplain to buy a Catholic flag and some meat. There's no one can hunt out
meat like him, sure as a sleepwalker. He can tell a
good piece of meat from the way his mouth waters.
A good thing they let me stay in the business. In
business you ask what price, not what religion. And

Protestant trousers keep you just as warm.

CHAPLAIN: As the mendicant monk said when there was talk of the Lutherans turning the whole world upside down: Beggars will *always* be needed. (MOTHER COURAGE *disappears into the wagon.*) She's worried about the cash box. Up to now they've ignored us—as if we were part of the wagon—but can it last?

SWISS CHEESE: I can get rid of it.

CHAPLAIN: That's almost *more* dangerous. Suppose you're seen. They have spies. Yesterday morning one jumped out of the very hole I was relieving myself in. I was so scared I almost broke out in prayer—*that* would have given me away all right! I believe their favorite way of finding a Protestant is smelling his excrement. The spy was a little brute with a bandage over one eye.

MOTHER COURAGE (*clambering out of the wagon with a basket*): I've found you out, you shameless hussy! (*She holds up* YVETTE's *red boots in triumph.*) Yvette's red boots! She just swiped them—because you went and told her she was a captivating person. (*She lays them in the basket.*) Stealing Yvette's boots! But *she* disgraces herself for money, *you* do it for nothing—for pleasure! I told you, you must wait for the peace. No soldiers! Save your proud peacock ways for peacetime!

CHAPLAIN: I don't find her proud.

MOTHER COURAGE: Prouder than she can afford to be. I like her when people say "I never noticed the poor thing." I like her when she's a stone in Dalarna, where there's nothing but stones. (*To* SWISS CHEESE:) Leave the cash box where it is, do you hear? And pay attention to your sister, she needs it. Between the two of you, you'll be the death of me yet. I'd rather take care of a bag of fleas.

She leaves with the CHAPLAIN. KATTRIN *clears the dishes away.*

SWISS CHEESE: Not many days more when you can sit in
the sun in your shirtsleeves. (KATTRIN *points to a
tree.*) Yes, the leaves are yellow already. (*With
gestures,* KATTRIN *asks if he wants a drink.*) I'm not
drinking, I'm thinking. (*Pause.*) She says she can't
sleep. So I *should* take the cash box away. I've
found a place for it. I'll keep it in the mole hole by
the river till the time comes. I might get it tonight
before sunrise and take it to the regiment. How far
can they have fled in three days? The Sergeant's
eyes'll pop out of his head. "I give you the cash box
to take care of, and what do you do," he'll say, "but
hand it right back to me: you've disappointed me
most pleasantly, Swiss Cheese." Yes, Kattrin, I *will*
have a glass now!

When KATTRIN *reappears behind the wagon two men
confront her. One of them is a* SERGEANT. *The other
doffs his hat and flourishes it in a showy greeting. He
has a bandage over one eye.*

MAN WITH THE BANDAGE: Good morning, young lady.
Have you seen a man from the Second Protestant
Regiment?

Terrified, KATTRIN *runs away, spilling her brandy.
The two men look at each other and then withdraw
after seeing* SWISS CHEESE.

SWISS CHEESE (*starting up from his reflection*): You're
spilling it! What's the matter with you, have you
hurt your eye? I don't understand. Yes, and I must
be going, too. I've decided it's the thing to do. (*He
stands up. She does all she can to make him aware
of the danger he is in. He only pushes her away.*) I'd
like to know what you mean. I know you mean well,
poor thing, you just can't get it out. And don't
trouble yourself about the brandy, I'll live to drink
so much of it, what's one glass? (*He takes the cash
box out of the wagon and puts it under his coat.*)

I'll be back right away. But don't hold me up or I'll
have to scold you. Yes, I know you mean well. If
you could only speak!

*When she tries to hold him back he kisses her and
pulls himself free. Exit. She is desperate and runs up
and down, emitting little sounds.* MOTHER COURAGE
and the CHAPLAIN *return.* KATTRIN *rushes at her
mother.*

MOTHER COURAGE: What *is* it, what *is* it, Kattrin? Control
yourself! Has someone done something to you?
Where is Swiss Cheese? (*To the* CHAPLAIN:) Don't
stand around, get that Catholic flag up! (*She takes a
Catholic flag out of her basket and the* CHAPLAIN *runs
it up the pole.*)

CHAPLAIN (*bitterly*): All good Catholics forever!

MOTHER COURAGE: Now, Kattrin, calm down and tell all
about it, your mother understands you. What, that
little bastard of mine's taken the cash box away?
I'll box his ears for him, the rascal! Now take your
time and don't try to talk, use your hands. I don't
like it when you howl like a dog, what'll the chaplain
think of you? You're giving him the creeps. A man
with one eye was here?

CHAPLAIN: That fellow with one eye is an informer! Have
they caught Swiss Cheese? (KATTRIN *shakes her
head, shrugs her shoulders.*) This is the end.

Voices off. The two men bring in SWISS CHEESE.

SWISS CHEESE: Let me go. I've nothing on me. You're
breaking my shoulder! I am innocent.

SERGEANT: This is where he comes from. These are his
friends.

MOTHER COURAGE: Us? Since when?

SWISS CHEESE: I don't even know 'em. I was just getting
my lunch here. Ten hellers it cost me. Maybe you
saw me sitting on that bench. It was too salty.

SERGEANT: Who *are* you people, anyway?

MOTHER COURAGE: Law-abiding citizens! It's true what he says. He bought his lunch here. And it was too salty.

SERGEANT: Are you pretending you don't know him?

MOTHER COURAGE: I can't know all of them, can I? *I* don't ask, "What's your name and are you a heathen?" If they pay up, they're not heathens to me. Are you a heathen?

SWISS CHEESE: Oh, no!

CHAPLAIN: He sat there like a law-abiding fellow and never once opened his mouth. Except to eat. Which is necessary.

SERGEANT: Who do you think *you* are?

MOTHER COURAGE: Oh, he's my barman. And you're thirsty, I'll bring you a glass of brandy. You must be footsore and weary!

SERGEANT: No brandy on duty. (*To* SWISS CHEESE:) You were carrying something. You must have hidden it by the river. We saw the bulge in your shirt.

MOTHER COURAGE: Sure it was him?

SWISS CHEESE: I think you mean another fellow. There *was* a fellow with something under his shirt, I saw him. I'm the wrong man.

MOTHER COURAGE: I think so too. It's a misunderstanding. Could happen to anyone. Oh, I know what people are like, I'm Mother Courage, you've heard of me, everyone knows about me, and I can tell you this: he looks honest.

SERGEANT: We're after the regimental cash box. And we know what the man looks like who's been keeping it. We've been looking for him two days. It's you.

SWISS CHEESE: No, it's not!

SERGEANT: And if you don't shell out, you're dead, see? Where is it?

MOTHER COURAGE (*urgently*): 'Course he'd give it to you to save his life. He'd up and say, *I've* got it, here it is, you're stronger than me. He's not *that* stupid. Speak, little stupid, the sergeant's giving you a chance!

SWISS CHEESE: What if I haven't got it?

SERGEANT: Come with us. We'll get it out of you. (*They take him off.*)

MOTHER COURAGE (*shouting after them*): He'd tell you! He's not *that* stupid! And don't you break his shoulder! (*She runs after them.*)

The same evening. The CHAPLAIN *and* KATTRIN *are rinsing glasses and polishing knives.*

CHAPLAIN: Cases of people getting caught like this are by no means unknown in the history of religion. I am reminded of the Passion of Our Lord and Savior. There's an old song about it.

He sings "The Song of the Hours":

> In the first hour of the day
> Simple Jesus Christ was
> Presented as a murderer
> To the heathen Pilate.
>
> Pilate found no fault in him
> No cause to condemn him
> So he sent the Lord away.
> Let King Herod see him!
>
> Hour the third: the Son of God
> Was with scourges beaten
> And they set a crown of thorns
> On the head of Jesus.
>
> And they dressed him as a king
> Joked and jested at him
> And the cross to die upon
> He himself must carry.
>
> Six: they stripped Lord Jesus bare.
> To the cross they nailed him.
> When the blood came gushing, he
> Prayed and loud lamented.

Each upon his cross, two thieves
Mocked him like the others.
And the bright sun crept away
Not to see such doings.

Nine: Lord Jesus cried aloud
That he was forsaken!
In a sponge upon a pole
Vinegar was fed him.

Then the Lord gave up the ghost
And the earth did tremble.
Temple curtains split in twain.
Cliffs fell in the ocean.

Evening: they broke the bones
Of the malefactors.
Then they took a spear and pierced
The side of gentle Jesus.

And the blood and water ran
And they laughed at Jesus.
Of this simple son of man
Such and more they tell us.

MOTHER COURAGE (*entering, excited*): It's life and death.
But the Sergeant will still listen to us. The only thing
is, he mustn't know it's our Swiss Cheese, or they'll
say we helped him. It's only a matter of money, but
where can *we* get money? Isn't Yvette here yet? I
talked to her on the way over. She's picked up a
Colonel who may be willing to buy her a canteen
business.

CHAPLAIN: You'd sell the wagon, everything?

MOTHER COURAGE: Where else would I get the money for
the Sergeant?

CHAPLAIN: What are you to live off?

MOTHER COURAGE: That's just it.

Enter YVETTE *with a hoary old* COLONEL.

YVETTE (*embracing* MOTHER COURAGE): *Dear* Mistress
Courage, we meet again. (*Whispering:*) He didn't
say no. (*Aloud:*) This is my friend, my, um, business
adviser. I happened to hear you might sell your
wagon. Due to special circumstances, I'd like to
think about it.

MOTHER COURAGE: I want to pawn it, not sell it. And
nothing hasty. In war time you don't find another
wagon like that so easy.

YVETTE (*disappointed*): Only pawn it? I thought you
wanted to sell. I don't know if I'm interested. (*To the*
COLONEL:) What do *you* think, my dear?

COLONEL: I quite agree with you, bunny.

MOTHER COURAGE: It's only for pawn.

YVETTE: I thought you *had* to have the money.

MOTHER COURAGE (*firmly*): I do have to have it. But I'd
rather wear my feet off looking for an offer than just
sell. Why? We live off the wagon. It's an opportunity
for you, Yvette. Who knows when you'll have another such? Who knows when you'll find another
business adviser?

COLONEL: Take it, take it!

YVETTE: My friend thinks I should go ahead, but I'm not
sure, if it's only for pawn. You think we should buy
it outright, don't you?

COLONEL: I do, bunny, I do!

MOTHER COURAGE: Then you must go and find something
that's for sale. Maybe you'll find it—if you have the
time, and your friend goes with you, let's say in about
a week, or two weeks, you may find the right thing.

YVETTE: Yes, we can certainly look around for something. I love going around looking, I love going
around with you, Poldy . . .

COLONEL: Really? Do you?

YVETTE: Oh, it's lovely! I could take two weeks of it!

COLONEL: Really, could you?

YVETTE: If you get the money, when are you thinking of paying it back?

MOTHER COURAGE: In two weeks. Maybe one.

YVETTE: I can't make up my mind. Poldy, advise me, *chéri!* (*She takes the* COLONEL *to one side.*) She'll *have* to sell, don't worry. That Lieutenant—the blond one, you know the one I mean—he'll lend me the money. He's *mad* about me, he says I remind him of someone. What do you advise?

COLONEL: Oh. I have to warn you against *him.* He's no good. He'll exploit the situation. I told you, bunny, I told you *I'd* buy you something, didn't I tell you that?

YVETTE: I simply can't let you!

COLONEL: Oh, please, please!

YVETTE: Well, if you think the Lieutenant might exploit the situation I *will* let you!

COLONEL: I do think so.

YVETTE: So you advise me to?

COLONEL: I do, bunny, I do!

YVETTE (*returning to* MOTHER COURAGE): My friend says all right. Write me out a receipt saying the wagon's mine when the two weeks are up—with everything in it. I'll just run through it all now, the two hundred guilders can wait. (*To the* COLONEL:) You go ahead to the camp, I'll follow, I must go over all this so nothing'll be missing later from *my* wagon!

COLONEL: Wait, I'll help you up! (*He does so.*) Come soon, honey bun! (*Exit.*)

MOTHER COURAGE: Yvette, Yvette!

YVETTE: There aren't many boots left!

MOTHER COURAGE: Yvette, this is no time to go through the wagon, yours or not yours. You promised you'd talk to the Sergeant about Swiss Cheese. There isn't a minute to lose. He's up before the court-martial one hour from now.

YVETTE: I just want to count these shirts again.

MOTHER COURAGE (*dragging her down the steps by the*

skirt): You hyena, Swiss Cheese's life's at stake! And don't say who the money comes from. Pretend he's your sweetheart, for heaven's sake, or we'll all get it for helping him.

YVETTE: I've arranged to meet One Eye in the bushes. He must be there by now.

CHAPLAIN: And don't hand over all two hundred, a hundred and fifty's sure to be enough.

MOTHER COURAGE: Is it your money? I'll thank you to keep your nose out of this, I'm not doing *you* out of your porridge. Now run, and no haggling, remember his life's at stake. (*She pushes* YVETTE *off.*)

CHAPLAIN: I didn't want to talk you into anything, but what are we going to live on? You have an unemployable daughter around your neck.

MOTHER COURAGE: I'm counting on that cash box, smart aleck. They'll pay his expenses out of it.

CHAPLAIN: You think she can work it?

MOTHER COURAGE: It's in her own interest: I pay the two hundred and she gets the wagon. She knows what she's doing, she won't have her Colonel on the string forever. Kattrin, go and clean the knives, use pumice stone. And don't *you* stand around like Jesus in Gethsemane. Get a move on, wash those glasses. There'll be over fifty cavalrymen here tonight, and you'll be saying you're not used to being on your feet. "Oh my poor feet, in church I never had to run around like this!" I think they'll let us have him. Thanks be to God they're corruptible. They're not wolves, they're human and after money. God is merciful, and men are bribable, that's how His will is done on earth as it is in Heaven. Corruption is our only hope. As long as there's corruption, there'll be merciful judges and even the innocent may get off.

YVETTE *comes in panting.*

YVETTE: They'll do it for two hundred if you make it snappy—these things change from one minute to the

next. I'd better take One Eye to my Colonel at once.
He confessed he had the cash box, they put the
thumbscrews on him. But he threw it in the river
when he noticed them coming up behind him. So it's
gone. Shall I run and get the money from my
Colonel?

MOTHER COURAGE: The cash box gone? How'll I ever get
my two hundred back?

YVETTE: So you thought you could get it from the cash
box? I *would* have been sunk. Not a hope, Mother
Courage. If you want your Swiss Cheese, you'll have
to pay. Or should I let the whole thing drop, so you
can keep your wagon?

MOTHER COURAGE: I wasn't figuring on this. But you
needn't hound me, you'll get the wagon, it's yours
already, and it's been mine seventeen years. I need
a minute to think it over, it's all so sudden. What can
I do? I *can't* pay two hundred. You *should* have
haggled with them. I must hold on to something, or
any passer-by can kick me in the ditch. Go and say
I'll pay a hundred and twenty or the deal's off. Even
then I lose the wagon.

YVETTE: They won't do it. And anyway, One Eye's in a
hurry. He keeps looking over his shoulder all the
time, he's so worked up. Hadn't I better give them
the whole two hundred?

MOTHER COURAGE (*desperate*): I can't pay it! I've been
working thirty years. She's twenty-five and still no
husband. I have her to think of. So leave me alone.
I know what I'm doing. A hundred and twenty or no
deal.

YVETTE: You know best. (*She runs off.*)

MOTHER COURAGE *turns away and slowly walks a few
paces to the rear. Then she turns around, looks
neither at the* CHAPLAIN *nor her daughter, and sits
down to help* KATTRIN *polish the knives.*

MOTHER COURAGE: Don't break the glasses, they're not

ours. Watch what you're doing, you're cutting yourself. Swiss Cheese will be back, I'll give two hundred,
if I have to. You'll get your brother back. With
eighty guilders we could pack a hamper with goods
and begin again. It wouldn't be the end of the world.

CHAPLAIN: The Bible says: the Lord will provide.

MOTHER COURAGE: Rub them dry, I said.

They clean the knives in silence.

They say the war will stop soon. How would it? I
ask. And no one can answer me. (*Slowly.*) The King
and the Pope are mortal enemies, their Faith is different. They must go for each other till one of them
drops dead, neither of them can relax till then. Even
so they can't get on with it. Why not? The Emperor
is in the way, and they both have something against
him. They're not going to fight each other to the
death with the Emperor lurking about till they're half
dead so he can fall on both of 'em! No, they're band-
ing together against the Emperor so he'll drop dead
first and they can go for each other.

Suddenly KATTRIN *runs sobbing behind the wagon.*

Someone once offered me five hundred guilders for
the wagon. I didn't take it. My Eilif, wherever he may
be, thought I'd taken it and cried all night.

YVETTE *comes running in.*

YVETTE: They won't do it. I warned you. One Eye was
going to drop it then and there. There's no point, he
said. He said the drums would roll any second now
and that's the sign a verdict has been reached. I
offered a hundred and fifty, he didn't even shrug. I
could hardly get him to stay there while I came
here.

MOTHER COURAGE: Tell him I'll pay two hundred. Run!

YVETTE *runs.* MOTHER COURAGE *sits, silent. The*

CHAPLAIN *has stopped doing the glasses.*

I believe—I've haggled too long.

In the distance, a roll of drums. The CHAPLAIN *stands up and walks toward the rear.* MOTHER COURAGE *remains seated. It grows dark. It gets light again.* MOTHER COURAGE *has not moved.* YVETTE *appears, pale.*

YVETTE: Now you've done it—with your haggling. You can keep the wagon now. He got eleven bullets in him. I don't know why I still bother about you, you don't deserve it, but I just happened to learn they don't think the cash box is really in the river. They suspect it's here, they think you're connected with him. I think they're going to bring him here to see if you'll give yourself away when you see him. You'd better not know him or we're in for it. And I'd better tell you straight, they're just behind me. Shall I keep Kattrin away? (MOTHER COURAGE *shakes her head.*) Does she know? Maybe she never heard the drums or didn't understand.

MOTHER COURAGE: She knows. Bring her.

YVETTE *brings* KATTRIN, *who walks over to her mother and stands by her.* MOTHER COURAGE *takes her hand. Two men come on with a stretcher; there is a sheet on it and something underneath. Beside them, the* SERGEANT. *They put the stretcher down.*

SERGEANT: Here's a man we can't identify. But he has to be registered to keep the records straight. He bought a meal from you. Look at him, see if you know him. (*He pulls back the sheet.*) Do you know him? (MOTHER COURAGE *shakes her head.*) What? You never saw him before he took that meal? (MOTHER COURAGE *shakes her head.*) Lift him up. Throw him in the carrion pit. He has no one that knows him.

They carry him off.

4

Mother Courage sings "The Song of the Great Capitulation."

Outside an officer's tent. MOTHER COURAGE *waits. A* CLERK
looks out of the tent.

CLERK: I know you. You had a Protestant paymaster with
you, he was hiding out with you. Better make no
complaint.

MOTHER COURAGE: But I'm innocent and if I give up it'll
look as if I have a bad conscience. They cut every-
think in my wagon to ribbons with their sabers and
then claimed a fine of five thalers for nothing and
less than nothing.

CLERK: For your own good, keep your trap shut. We
haven't many canteens, so we let you stay in business,
especially if you've a bad conscience and have to pay
a fine now and then.

MOTHER COURAGE: I'm going to file a complaint.

CLERK: As you wish. Wait here till the Captain has time.
(*He withdraws into the tent.*)

A YOUNG SOLDIER *comes storming in.*

YOUNG SOLDIER: Screw the Captain! Where *is* the son of
a bitch? Swiping my reward, spending it on brandy
for his whores, I'll rip his belly open!

AN OLDER SOLDIER (*coming after him*): Shut your hole,
you'll wind up in the stocks.

YOUNG SOLDIER: Come out, you thief, I'll make lamb
chops out of you! I was the only one in the squad
who swam the river and *he* grabs my money, I can't
even buy myself a beer. Come on out! And let me
slice you up!

OLDER SOLDIER: Holy Christ, he'll destroy himself!

YOUNG SOLDIER: Let me go or I'll run *you* down too. This has got to be settled!

OLDER SOLDIER: Saved the Colonel's horse and didn't get the reward. He's young, he hasn't been at it long.

MOTHER COURAGE: Let him go. He doesn't have to be chained, he's not a dog. Very reasonable to want a reward. Why else should he want to shine?

YOUNG SOLDIER: He's in there pouring it down! You're all nice. I've done something special, I want the reward!

MOTHER COURAGE: Young man, don't scream at *me,* I have my own troubles. And go easy with your voice, you may need it when the Captain comes. The Captain'll come and you'll be hoarse and can't make a sound, so he'll have to deny himself the pleasure of sticking you in the stocks till you pass out. The screamers don't scream long, only half an hour, after which they have to be sung to sleep, they're all in.

YOUNG SOLDIER: I'm not all in, and sleep's out of the question. I'm hungry. They're making their bread out of acorns and hempseed, and not even much of that. He's whoring on my money, and I'm hungry. I'll murder him!

MOTHER COURAGE: I understand: you're hungry. Last year your Commander ordered you people out of the streets and into the fields. So the crops got trampled down. I could have got ten guilders for boots, if anyone'd had ten guilders, and if I'd had any boots. He didn't expect to be around this year, but he is, and there's famine. I understand: you're angry.

YOUNG SOLDIER: It's no use your talking. I won't stand for injustice!

MOTHER COURAGE: You're quite right. But how long? How long won't you stand for injustice? One hour? Or two? You haven't asked yourself that, have you? And yet it's the main thing. It's pure misery to sit in the stocks. Especially if you leave it till then to decide you do stand for injustice.

YOUNG SOLDIER: I don't know why I listen to you. Screw that Captain! Where is he?

MOTHER COURAGE: You listen because you know I'm right. Your rage has calmed down already. It was a short one and you'd need a long one. But where would you find it?

YOUNG SOLDIER: Are you trying to say it's not right to ask for the money?

MOTHER COURAGE: Just the opposite. I only say, your rage won't last. You'll get nowhere with it, it's a pity. If your rage was a long one, I'd urge you on. Slice him up, I'd advise you. But what's the use if you *don't* slice him up because you can feel your tail between your legs? You stand there and the Captain lets you have it.

OLDER SOLDIER: You're quite right, he's crazy.

YOUNG SOLDIER: All right, we'll see whether I slice him up or not. (*He draws his sword.*) When he comes out, I slice him up!

CLERK (*looking out*): The Captain will be out in a minute. (*In the tone of military command:*) Be seated!

The YOUNG SOLDIER *sits.*

MOTHER COURAGE: And he *is* seated. What did I tell you? You are seated. They know us through and through. They know how they must work it. Be seated! And we sit. And in sitting there's no revolt. Better not stand up again—not the way you did before—don't stand up again. And don't be embarrassed in front of me, I'm no better, not a scrap. They've drawn our teeth, haven't they? If we say boo, it's bad for business. Let me tell you about the great capitulation.

She sings "The Song of the Great Capitulation":

> Long ago when I was a green beginner
> I believed I was a special case.

(None of your ordinary run of the mill girls, with my looks and my talent, and my love of the higher things in life!)

And if I picked a hair out of my dinner
I would put the cook right in his place.

(All or nothing. Anyhow, never the second best. I am the master of my Fate. I'll take no orders from no one.)

Then a little bird whispered in my ear:
"That's all very well, but wait a year
And you will join the big brass band
And with your trumpet in your hand
You'll march in lockstep with the rest.
Then one day, look! The battalions wheel!
The whole thing swings from east to west!
And falling on your knees, you'll squeal:
The Lord God, He knows best!
(But don't give *me* that!)"

And a month or two before that year was over
I had learned to drink their cup of tea.

(Two children round your neck, and the price of bread and what all!)

And the day soon came when I was to discover
They had me just where they wanted me.

(You must get in good with people. If you scratch my back, I'll scratch yours. Don't stick your neck out.)

And that little bird whispered in my ear:
"You didn't even take a year!
And you have joined the big brass band
And with your trumpet in your hand
You marched in lockstep with the rest.
But one day, look! The battalions wheeled!
The whole thing swung from east to west!
And falling on your knees, you squealed:

The Lord God, He knows best!
(But don't give *me* that!)"

Yes, our hopes are high, our plans colossal!
And we hitch our wagon to a star!

(Where there's a will there's a way. One can't hold a
good man down.)

We can move mountains, says St. Paul the great
　　Apostle
And yet: how heavy one cigar!

(We must cut our coat according to our cloth.)

For that little bird whispers in your ear:
"That's all very well but wait a year
And we will join the big brass band
And with our trumpet in our hand
We march in lockstep with the rest.
But one day, look! The battalions wheel!
The whole thing swings from east to west!
And falling on our knees, we squeal:
The Lord God, He knows best!
(But don't give *me* that!)"

And so I think you should stay here with your sword
drawn if you're set on it and your anger is big enough.
You have good cause, I admit. But if your anger is a
short one, you'd better go.

YOUNG SOLDIER: Kiss my ass. (*He stumbles off, the other*
SOLDIER *following him.*)

CLERK (*sticking his head out*): The Captain is ready now.
You can file your complaint.

MOTHER COURAGE: I've thought better of it. I'm not com-
plaining. (*Exit.*)

The CLERK *looks after her, shaking his head.*

5

Two years have passed. The war covers wider and wider territory. Forever on the move, the little wagon crosses Poland, Moravia, Bavaria, Italy, and again Bavaria. 1631. Tilly's victory at Magdeburg costs Mother Courage four officers' shirts.

The wagon stands in a war-ravaged village. Faint military music from the distance. Two SOLDIERS *are being served at a counter by* KATTRIN *and* MOTHER COURAGE. *One of them has a woman's fur coat about his shoulders.*

MOTHER COURAGE: What, you can't pay? No money, no brandy! They can play victory marches, they should pay their men.

FIRST SOLDIER: I want my brandy! I arrived too late for plunder. The Chief allowed one hour to plunder the town, it's a swindle. He's not inhuman, he says. So I suppose they bought him off.

CHAPLAIN (*staggering in*): There are more in the farmhouse. A family of peasants. Help me someone. I need linen!

The second SOLDIER *goes with him.* KATTRIN *is getting very excited. She tries to get her mother to bring linen out.*

MOTHER COURAGE: I have none. I sold all my bandages to the regiment. I'm not tearing up my officers' shirts for these people.

CHAPLAIN (*calling over his shoulder*): I said I need linen!

MOTHER COURAGE (*stopping* KATTRIN *from entering the wagon*): Not a thing! They can't pay, and why? They have nothing and they pay nothing!

70

CHAPLAIN (*to a* WOMAN *he is carrying in*): Why did you stay out there in the line of fire?

WOMAN: Our farm—

MOTHER COURAGE: Think they'd ever let go of *anything*? And now I'm supposed to pay. Well, I won't!

FIRST SOLDIER: They're Protestants, why should they be Protestants?

MOTHER COURAGE: Protestant, Catholic, what do *they* care? Their farm's gone, that's what.

SECOND SOLDIER: They're not Protestants anyway, they're Catholics.

FIRST SOLDIER: In a bombardment we can't pick and choose.

A PEASANT (*brought on by the* CHAPLAIN): My arm's gone.

CHAPLAIN: Where's that linen?

All look at MOTHER COURAGE, *who does not budge.*

MOTHER COURAGE: I can't give you any. With all I have to pay out—taxes, duties, bribes.... (KATTRIN *takes up a board and threatens her mother with it, emitting gurgling sounds.*) Are you out of your mind? Put that board down or I'll let you have one, you lunatic! I'm giving nothing, I don't dare, I have myself to think of. (*The* CHAPLAIN *lifts her bodily off the steps of the wagon and sets her down on the ground. He takes out shirts from the wagon and tears them in strips.*) My shirts, my officers' shirts!

From the house comes the cry of a child in pain.

PEASANT: The child's still in there.

KATTRIN *runs in.*

CHAPLAIN (*to the* WOMAN): Stay where you are. She's getting it for you.

MOTHER COURAGE: Hold her back, the roof may fall in!

CHAPLAIN: I'm not going back in there!

MOTHER COURAGE (*pulled in both directions*): Go easy on my expensive linen.

The SECOND SOLDIER *holds her back.* KATTRIN *brings a baby out of the ruins.*

MOTHER COURAGE: Another baby to drag around, you must be pleased with yourself. Give it to its mother this minute! Or do I have to fight you again for hours till I get it from you? Are you deaf? (*To the* SECOND SOLDIER:) Don't stand about gawking, go back there and tell 'em to stop that music, I can see their victory without it. I have nothing but losses from your victory!

CHAPLAIN (*bandaging*): The blood's coming through.

KATTRIN *is rocking the child and half humming a lullaby.*

MOTHER COURAGE: There she sits, happy as a lark in all this misery. Give the baby back, the mother is coming to! (*She sees the* FIRST SOLDIER. *He had been handling the drinks, and is now trying to make off with the bottle.*) God's truth! You beast! You want another victory, do you? Then pay for it!

FIRST SOLDIER: I have nothing.

MOTHER COURAGE (*snatching the fur coat back*): Then leave this coat, it's stolen goods anyhow.

CHAPLAIN: There's still someone in there.

6

Before the city of Ingolstadt in Bavaria Mother Courage is present at the funeral of the fallen commander, Tilly. Conversations take place about war heroes and the duration of the war. The Chaplain complains that his talents are lying fallow and Kattrin gets the red boots. The year is 1632.

The inside of a canteen tent. The inner side of a counter at the rear. Rain. In the distance, drums and funeral music. The CHAPLAIN *and the regimental* CLERK *are playing draughts.* MOTHER COURAGE *and her daughter are taking an inventory.*

CHAPLAIN: The funeral procession is just starting out.

MOTHER COURAGE: Pity about the Chief—twenty-two pairs of socks—getting killed that way. They say it was an accident. There was a fog over the fields that morning, and the fog was to blame. The Chief called up another regiment, told 'em to fight to the death, rode back again, missed his way in the fog, went forward instead of back, and ran smack into a bullet in the thick of battle—only four lanterns left. (*A whistle from the rear. She goes to the counter. To a* SOLDIER:) It's a disgrace the way you're all skipping your Commander's funeral! (*She pours a drink.*)

CLERK: They shouldn't have handed the money out before the funeral. Now the men are all getting drunk instead of going to it.

CHAPLAIN (*to the* CLERK): Don't you have to be there?

CLERK: I stayed away because of the rain.

MOTHER COURAGE: It's different for you, the rain might spoil your uniform. I hear they wanted to ring the

73

bells for his funeral, which is natural, but it came out that the churches had been shot up by his orders, so the poor Commander won't be hearing any bells when they lower him in his grave. Instead, they'll fire off three shots so the occasion won't be *too* sober—sixteen leather belts.

A VOICE FROM THE COUNTER: Service! One brandy!

MOTHER COURAGE: Your money first. No, you *can't* come inside the tent, not with those boots on. You can drink outside, rain or no rain. I only let officers in here. (*To the* CLERK:) The Chief had his troubles lately, I hear. There was unrest in the Second Regiment because he didn't pay 'em. He said it was a war of religion and they must fight it free of charge.

Funeral march. All look toward the rear.

CHAPLAIN: Now they're filing past the body.

MOTHER COURAGE: I feel sorry for a Commander or an Emperor like that—when he might have had something special in mind, something they'd talk about in times to come, something they'd raise a statue to him for. The conquest of the world now, *that's* a goal for a Commander, he wouldn't know any better. . . . Lord, worms have got into the biscuits. . . . In short, he works his hands to the bone and then it's all spoiled by the common riffraff that only wants a jug of beer or a bit of company, not the higher things in life. The finest plans have always been spoiled by the littleness of them that should carry them out. Even Emperors can't do it all by themselves. They count on support from their soldiers and the people round about. Am I right?

CHAPLAIN (*laughing*): You're right, Mother Courage, till you come to the soldiers. They do what they can. Those fellows outside, for example, drinking their brandy in the rain, I'd trust 'em to fight a hundred years, one war after another, two at a time if necessary. And I wasn't trained as a commander.

MOTHER COURAGE: . . . Seventeen leather belts. . . . Then you don't think the war might end?

CHAPLAIN: Because a commander's dead? Don't be childish, they grow on trees. There are always heroes.

MOTHER COURAGE: Well, I wasn't asking for the sake of argument. I was wondering if I should buy up a lot of supplies. They happen to be cheap just now. But if the war ended, I might just as well throw them away.

CHAPLAIN: I realize you are serious, Mother Courage. Well, there've always been people going around saying some day the war will end. I say, you can't be sure the war will *ever* end. Of course it may have to pause occasionally—for breath, as it were—it can even meet with an accident—nothing on this earth is perfect—a war of which we could say it left nothing to be desired will probably never exist. A war can come to a sudden halt—from unforeseen causes— you can't think of everything—a little oversight, and the war's in the hole, and someone's got to pull it out again! The someone is the Emperor or the King or the Pope. They're such friends in need, the war has really nothing to worry about, it can look forward to a prosperous future.

A SOLDIER (*singing at the counter*):

> One schnapps, mine host, make haste!
> We have no time to waste:
> We must be shooting, shooting, shooting
> Our Emperor's foes uprooting!

Make it a double. This is a holiday.

MOTHER COURAGE: If I was sure you're right . . .

CHAPLAIN: Think it out for yourself: how *could* the war end?

SOLDIER (*off-stage*):

> Two breasts, mine host, make haste!
> For we have no time to waste:

We must be hating, hating, hating
We cannot keep our Emperor waiting!

CLERK (*suddenly*): What about peace? Yes, peace. I'm
from Bohemia. I'd like to get home once in a while.

CHAPLAIN: Oh, you would, would you? Dear old peace!
What happens to the hole when the cheese is gone?

SOLDIER (*off-stage*):

Your blessing, priest, make haste!
For we have no time to waste:
We must be dying, dying, dying
Our Emperor's greatness glorifying!

CLERK: In the long run you can't live without peace!

CHAPLAIN: Well, I'd say there's peace even in war, war
has its islands of peace. For war satisfies *all* needs,
even those of peace, yes, they're provided for, or the
war couldn't keep going. In war—as in the very thick
of peace—you can take a crap, and between one
battle and the next there's always a beer, and even
on the march you can snatch a nap—on your elbow
maybe, in a gutter—something can always be man-
aged. Of course you can't play cards during an
attack, but neither can you while ploughing the fields
in peace time: it's when the victory's won that there
are possibilities. You have your leg shot off, and at
first you raise quite an outcry as if it *was* something,
but soon you calm down or take a swig of brandy, and
you end up hopping about, and the war is none the
worse for your little misadventure. And can't you
be fruitful and multiply in the thick of slaughter—
behind a barn or somewhere? Nothing can keep you
from it very long in any event. And so the war has
your offspring and can carry on. War is like love, it
always finds a way. Why *should* it end?

KATTRIN *has stopped working. She stares at the*
CHAPLAIN.

MOTHER COURAGE: Then I *will* buy those supplies, I'll rely on you. (KATTRIN *suddenly bangs a basket of glasses down on the ground and runs out.* MOTHER COURAGE *laughs.*) Kattrin! Lord, Kattrin's still going to wait for peace. I promised her she'll get a husband—when it's peace. (*She runs after her.*)

CLERK (*standing up*): I win. You were talking. You pay.

MOTHER COURAGE (*returning with* KATTRIN): Be sensible, the war'll go on a bit longer, and we'll make a bit more money, then peace'll be all the nicer. Now you go into the town, it's not ten minutes walk, and bring the things from the Golden Lion, just the more expensive ones, we can get the rest later in the wagon. It's all arranged, the clerk will go with you, most of the soldiers are at the Commander's funeral, nothing can happen to you. Do a good job, don't lose anything, Kattrin, think of your trousseau!

KATTRIN *ties a cloth around her head and leaves with the* CLERK.

CHAPLAIN: You don't mind her going with the clerk?

MOTHER COURAGE: She's not so pretty anyone would want to ruin her.

CHAPLAIN: The way you run your business and always come through is highly commendable, Mother Courage—I see how you got your name.

MOTHER COURAGE: The poor need courage. Why? They're lost. That they even get up in the morning is something—in *their* plight. Or that they plough a field—in war time. Even their bringing children into the world shows they have courage, for they have no prospects. They have to hang each other one by one and slaughter each other in the lump, so if they want to look each other in the face once in a while, well, it takes courage. That they put up with an Emperor and a Pope, that takes an unnatural amount of courage, for *they* cost you your life. (*She sits, takes a*

small pipe from her pocket and smokes it.) You
might chop me a bit of firewood.

CHAPLAIN (*reluctantly taking his coat off and preparing
to chop wood*): Properly speaking, I'm a pastor of
souls, not a woodcutter.

MOTHER COURAGE: But I don't have a soul. And I do
need wood.

CHAPLAIN: What's that little pipe you've got there?

MOTHER COURAGE: Just a pipe.

CHAPLAIN: I think it's a very particular pipe.

MOTHER COURAGE: Oh?

CHAPLAIN: The cook's pipe in fact. The cook from the
Oxenstierna Regiment.

MOTHER COURAGE: If you know, why beat about the bush?

CHAPLAIN: Because I don't know if you've been *aware*
that's what you've been smoking. It was possible you
just rummaged among your belongings and your
fingers just lit on a pipe and you just took it. In pure
absent-mindedness.

MOTHER COURAGE: How do you know that's not it?

CHAPLAIN: It isn't. You *are* aware of it. (*He brings the ax
down on the block with a crash.*)

MOTHER COURAGE: What if I was?

CHAPLAIN: I must give you a warning, Mother Courage,
it's my duty. You are unlikely to see the gentleman
again but that's no pity, you're in luck. Mother
Courage, he did not impress me as trustworthy. On
the contrary.

MOTHER COURAGE: Really? He was such a nice man.

CHAPLAIN: Well! So that's what you call a nice man. I
do not. (*The ax falls again.*) Far be it from me to
wish him ill, but I cannot—cannot—describe him as
nice. No, no, he's a Don Juan, a cunning Don Juan.
Just look at that pipe if you don't believe me. You
must admit it tells all.

MOTHER COURAGE: I see nothing special in it. It's been
used, of course.

CHAPLAIN: It's bitten halfway through! He's a man of

great violence! It is the pipe of a man of great
violence, you can see *that* if you've any judgment
left! (*He deals the block a tremendous blow.*)

MOTHER COURAGE: Don't bite my chopping block halfway
through!

CHAPLAIN: I told you I had no training as a woodcutter.
The care of souls was my field. Around here my gifts
and capabilities are grossly misused. In physical labor
my God-given talents find no—um—adequate ex-
pression—which is a sin. You haven't heard me
preach. Why, I can put such spirit into a regiment
with a single sermon that the enemy's a mere flock of
sheep to them and their own lives no more than
smelly old shoes to be thrown away at the thought
of final victory! God has given me the gift of tongues.
I can preach you out of your senses!

MOTHER COURAGE: I need my senses. What would I do
without them?

CHAPLAIN: Mother Courage, I have often thought that—
under a veil of plain speech—you conceal a heart.
You are human, you need warmth.

MOTHER COURAGE: The best way of warming this tent is
to chop plenty of firewood.

CHAPLAIN: You're changing the subject. Seriously, my
dear Courage, I sometimes ask myself how it would
be if our relationship should be somewhat more
firmly cemented. I mean, now the wild wind of war
has whirled us so strangely together.

MOTHER COURAGE: The cement's pretty firm already. I
cook your meals. And you lend a hand—at chopping
firewood, for instance.

CHAPLAIN (*going over to her, gesturing with the ax*): You
know what I mean by a close relationship. It has
nothing to do with eating and woodcutting and such
base necessities. Let your heart speak!

MOTHER COURAGE: Don't come at me like that with your
ax, that'd be *too* close a relationship!

CHAPLAIN: This is no laughing matter, I am in earnest. I've thought it all over.

MOTHER COURAGE: Dear Chaplain, be a sensible fellow. I like you, and I don't want to heap coals of fire on your head. All I want is to bring me and my children through in that wagon. It isn't just mine, the wagon, and anyway I've no mind to start any adventures. At the moment I'm taking quite a risk buying these things when the Commander's fallen and there's all this talk of peace. Where would you go, if I was ruined? See? You don't even know. Now chop some firewood and it'll be warm of an evening, which is quite a lot in times like these. What was that? (*She stands up.* KATTRIN *enters, breathless, with a wound across the eye and forehead. She is dragging all sorts of articles, parcels, leather goods, a drum, etc.*) What is it, were you attacked? On the way back? She was attacked on the way back! I'll bet it was that soldier who got drunk on my liquor. I should never have let you go. Dump all that stuff! It's not bad, the wound is only a flesh wound. I'll bandage it for you, it'll all be healed up in a week. They're worse than animals. (*She bandages the wound.*)

CHAPLAIN: I reproach them with nothing. At home they never did these shameful things. The men who start the wars are responsible, they bring out the worst in people.

MOTHER COURAGE: Didn't the clerk walk you back home? That's because you're a respectable girl, he thought they'd leave you alone. The wound's not at all deep, it will never show. There: all bandaged up. Now, I've got something for you, rest easy. I've been keeping them secret. (*She digs* YVETTE's *red boots out of a bag.*) Well, what do you see? You always wanted them. Now you have them. (*She helps her to put the boots on.*) Put them on quick, before I change my mind. It will never show, though it wouldn't bother *me* if it did. The ones they like

fare worst. They drag them around till they're
finished. Those they don't care for they leave alone.
I've seen so many girls, pretty as they come in the
beginning, then all of a sudden they're so ugly they'd
scare a wolf. They can't even go behind a tree on
the street without having something to fear from
it. They lead a frightful life. Like with trees: the
tall, straight ones are cut down for roof timber, and
the crooked ones can enjoy life. So this wound here
is really a piece of luck. The boots have kept well.
I gave them a good cleaning before I put them away.

KATTRIN *leaves the boots and creeps into the wagon.*

CHAPLAIN (*when she's gone*): I hope she won't be dis-
figured?

MOTHER COURAGE: There'll be a scar. She needn't wait
for peace now.

CHAPLAIN: She didn't let them get any of the stuff.

MOTHER COURAGE: Maybe I shouldn't have made such
a point of it. If only I ever knew what went on inside her head. Once she stayed out all night, once
in all the years. Afterward she seemed much the
same, except that she worked harder. I could never
get out of her what happened. I worried about it
for quite a while. (*She picks up the things* KATTRIN
spilled and sorts them angrily.) This is war. A nice
source of income, I must say!

Cannon shots.

CHAPLAIN: Now they're lowering the Commander into
his grave! A historic moment.

MOTHER COURAGE: It's a historic moment to me when
they hit my daughter over the eye. She's all but
finished now, she'll never get a husband, and she's
so mad about children! Even her dumbness comes
from the war. A soldier stuck something in her
mouth when she was little. I'll never see Swiss Cheese
again, and where my Eilif is the Good Lord knows.
Curse the war!

7

Mother Courage at the height of her business career.

A highway. The CHAPLAIN, MOTHER COURAGE, *and her daughter* KATTRIN *pull the wagon, and new wares are hanging from it.* MOTHER COURAGE *wears a necklace of silver coins.*

MOTHER COURAGE: I won't let you spoil my war for me. Destroys the weak, does it? Well, what does peace do for 'em, huh? War feeds its people better.

She sings:

> If war don't suit your disposition
> When victory comes, you will be dead.
> War is a business proposition:
> But not with cheese, with steel instead!
>> Christians, awake! Winter is gone!
>> The snows depart! Dead men sleep on!
>> Let all of you who still survive
>> Get out of bed and look alive!

And staying in one place won't help either. Those who stay at home are the first to go.

She sings:

>> Too many seek a bed to sleep in:
>> Each ditch is taken, and each cave
>> And he who digs a hole to creep in
>> Finds he has dug an early grave.
>> And many a man spends many a minute
>> In hurrying toward some resting place.
>> You wonder, when at last he's in it
>> Just why the fellow forced the pace.

The wagon proceeds.

8

1632. In this same year Gustavus Adolphus fell in the battle of Lützen. The peace threatens Mother Courage with ruin. Her brave son performs one heroic deed too many and comes to a shameful end.

A camp. A summer morning. In front of the wagon, an OLD WOMAN *and her son. The son is dragging a large bag of bedding.*

MOTHER COURAGE (*from inside the wagon*): Must you come at the crack of dawn?

YOUNG MAN: We've been walking all night, twenty miles it was, we have to be back today.

MOTHER COURAGE (*still inside*): What do I want with bed feathers? People don't even have houses.

YOUNG MAN: At least wait till you see 'em.

OLD WOMAN: Nothing doing here either, let's go.

YOUNG MAN: And let 'em sign away the roof over our heads for taxes? Maybe she'll pay three guilders if you throw in that bracelet. (*Bells start ringing.*) You hear, mother?

VÒICES (*from the rear*): It's peace! The King of Sweden's been killed!

MOTHER COURAGE *sticks her head out of the wagon. She hasn't done her hair yet.*

MOTHER COURAGE: Bells! What are the bells for, middle of the week?

CHAPLAIN (*crawling out from under the wagon*): What's that they're shouting?

YOUNG MAN: It's peace.

CHAPLAIN: Peace!

MOTHER COURAGE: Don't tell me peace has broken out—
when I've just gone and bought all these supplies!

CHAPLAIN (*calling, toward the rear*): Is it peace?

VOICE (*from a distance*): They say the war stopped three
weeks ago. I've only just heard.

CHAPLAIN (*to* MOTHER COURAGE): Or why would they
ring the bells?

VOICE: A great crowd of Lutherans have just arrived with
wagons—they brought the news.

YOUNG MAN: It's peace, mother. (*The* OLD WOMAN *collapses.*) What's the matter?

MOTHER COURAGE (*back in the wagon*): Kattrin, it's
peace! Put on your black dress, we're going to
church, we owe it to Swiss Cheese! Can it be true?

YOUNG MAN: The people here say so too, the war's over.
Can you stand up? (*The* OLD WOMAN *stands up,
dazed.*) I'll get the harness shop going again now,
I promise you. Everything'll be all right, father will
get his bed back. . . . Can you walk? (*To the*
CHAPLAIN:) She felt ill, it was the news. She didn't
believe there'd ever be peace again. Father always
said there would. We're going home. (*They leave.*)

MOTHER COURAGE (*off*): Give her some brandy.

CHAPLAIN: They've left already.

MOTHER COURAGE (*still off*): What's going on in the
camp over there?

CHAPLAIN: They're all getting together. I think I'll go
over. Shall I put my pastor's coat on again?

MOTHER COURAGE: Better get the exact news first, and
not risk being taken for the Antichrist. I'm glad
about the peace even though I'm ruined. At least
I've got two of my children through the war. Now
I'll see my Eilif again.

CHAPLAIN: And who may this be coming down from the
camp? Well, if it isn't our Swedish Commander's
cook!

COOK (*somewhat bedraggled, carrying a bundle*): Who's
here? The chaplain!

CHAPLAIN: Mother Courage, a visitor!

MOTHER COURAGE *clambers out.*

COOK: Well, I promised I'd come over for a brief conversation as soon as I had time. I didn't forget your brandy, Mrs. Fierling.

MOTHER COURAGE: Jesus, the Commander's cook! After all these years! Where is Eilif, my eldest?

COOK: Isn't he here yet? He went on ahead yesterday, he was on his way over.

CHAPLAIN: I *will* put my pastor's coat on. I'll be back. (*He goes behind the wagon.*)

MOTHER COURAGE: He may be here any minute then. (*She calls toward the wagon:*) Kattrin, Eilif's coming! Bring a glass of brandy for the cook, Kattrin! (KATTRIN *doesn't come.*) Just pull your hair over it. Mr. Lamb is no stranger. (*She gets the brandy herself.*) She won't come out. Peace is nothing to her, it was too long coming. They hit her right over the eye. You can hardly see it now. But she thinks people stare at her.

COOK: Ah yes, war! (*He and* MOTHER COURAGE *sit.*)

MOTHER COURAGE: Cook, you come at a bad time: I'm ruined.

COOK: What? That's terrible!

MOTHER COURAGE: The peace has broken my neck. On the chaplain's advice I've gone and bought a lot of supplies. Now everybody's leaving and I'm holding the baby.

COOK: How could you listen to the chaplain? If I'd had time—but the Catholics were too quick for me— I'd have warned you against him. He's a windbag. Well, so now he's the big man round here!

MOTHER COURAGE: He's been doing the dishes for me and helping with the wagon.

COOK: With the wagon—him! And I'll bet he's told you a few of his jokes. He has a most unhealthy attitude to women. I tried to influence him but it was no good. He isn't sound.

MOTHER COURAGE: Are you sound?

COOK: If I'm nothing else, I'm sound. Your health!

MOTHER COURAGE: Sound! Only one person around here was ever sound, and I never had to slave as I did then. He sold the blankets off the children's beds in the spring, and he called my harmonica unchristian. You aren't recommending yourself if you *admit* you're sound.

COOK: You fight tooth and nail, don't you? I like that.

MOTHER COURAGE: Don't tell me you've been dreaming of my teeth and nails.

COOK: Well, here we sit, while the bells of peace do ring, and you pouring your famous brandy as only you know how!

MOTHER COURAGE: I don't think much of the bells of peace at the moment. I don't see how they can hand out all this pay that's in arrears. And then where shall I be with my famous brandy? Have you all been paid?

COOK (*hesitating*): Not exactly. That's why we disbanded. In the circumstances, I thought, why stay? For the time being, I'll look up a couple of friends. So here I sit—with you.

MOTHER COURAGE: In other words, you're broke.

COOK (*annoyed by the bells*): It's about time they stopped that racket! I'd like to set myself up in some business. I'm fed up with being their cook. I'm supposed to make do with tree roots and shoe leather, and then they throw my hot soup in my face! Being a cook nowadays is a dog's life. I'd sooner be a soldier, but of course, it's peace now. (*As the* CHAPLAIN *turns up, wearing his old coat:*) We'll talk it over later.

CHAPLAIN: The coat's pretty good. Just a few moth holes.

COOK: I don't know why you take the trouble. You won't find another pulpit. Who could you incite now to earn an honest living or risk his life for a cause? Besides. I have a bone to pick with you.

CHAPLAIN: Have you?

COOK: I have. You advised a lady to buy superfluous goods on the pretext that the war would never end.

CHAPLAIN (*hotly*): I'd like to know what business it is of yours?

COOK: It's unprincipled behavior! How can you give unwanted advice? And interfere with the conduct of other people's business?

CHAPLAIN: Who's interfering now, I'd like to know? (*To* MOTHER COURAGE:) I had no idea you were such a close friend of this gentleman and had to account to *him* for everything.

MOTHER COURAGE: Now don't get excited. The cook's giving his personal opinion. You can't deny your war was a flop.

CHAPLAIN: You have no respect for peace, Courage. You're a hyena of the battlefield!

MOTHER COURAGE: A what?

COOK: Who insults my girl friend insults me!

CHAPLAIN: I am *not* speaking to you, your intentions are only too transparent! (*To* MOTHER COURAGE:) But when I see *you* take peace between finger and thumb like a snotty old hanky, my humanity rebels! It shows that you want war, not peace, for what you get out of it. But don't forget the proverb: he who sups with the devil must use a long spoon!

MOTHER COURAGE: Remember what one fox said to another that was caught in a trap? "If you stay there, you're just asking for trouble!" There isn't much love lost between me and the war. And when it comes to calling me a hyena, you and I part company.

CHAPLAIN: Then why all this grumbling about the peace just as everyone's heaving a sigh of relief? Is it for the junk in your wagon?

MOTHER COURAGE: My goods are not junk. I live off them. *You've* been living off them.

CHAPLAIN: You live off war. Exactly.

COOK (*to the* CHAPLAIN): As a grown man, you should know better than to go around advising people. (*To* MOTHER COURAGE:) Now, in your situation you'd be smart to get rid of certain goods at once—before the prices sink to nothing. Get ready and get going, there isn't a moment to lose!

MOTHER COURAGE: That's sensible advice, I think I'll take it.

CHAPLAIN: Because the cook says so.

MOTHER COURAGE: Why didn't *you* say so? He's right, I must get to the market. (*She climbs into the wagon.*)

COOK: One up for me, Chaplain. You have no presence of mind. You should have said, "*I* gave you advice? Why, I was just talking politics!" And you shouldn't take me on as a rival. Cockfights are not becoming to your cloth.

CHAPLAIN: If you don't shut your trap, I'll murder you, cloth or no cloth!

COOK (*taking his boots off and unwinding the wrappings on his feet*): If you hadn't degenerated into a godless tramp, you could easily get yourself a parsonage, now it's peace. Cooks won't be needed, there's nothing to cook, but there's still plenty to believe, and people will go right on believing it.

CHAPLAIN: Mr. Lamb, please don't drive me out! Since I became a tramp, I'm a somewhat better man. I couldn't preach to 'em any more.

YVETTE POTTIER *enters, decked out in black, with a stick. She is much older, fatter, and heavily powdered. Behind her, a* SERVANT.

YVETTE: Hullo, everybody! Is this Mother Courage's establishment?

CHAPLAIN: Quite right. And with whom have we the pleasure?

YVETTE: 1 am Madame Colonel Starhemberg, good people. Where's Mother Courage?

CHAPLAIN (*calling to the wagon*): Madame Colonel Starhemberg wants to speak to you!

MOTHER COURAGE (*from inside*): Coming!

YVETTE (*calling*): It's Yvette!

MOTHER COURAGE (*inside*): Yvette!

YVETTE: Just to see how you're getting on! (*As the* COOK *turns around in horror*:) Peter!

COOK: Yvette!

YVETTE: Of all things! How did *you* get here?

COOK: On a cart.

CHAPLAIN: Well! You know each other? Intimately?

YVETTE: I'll say. (*Scrutinizing the* COOK:) You're fat.

COOK: For that matter, *you're* no beanpole.

YVETTE: Anyway, it's lucky we've met, tramp. Now I can tell you what I think of you.

CHAPLAIN: Do so, tell him all, but wait till Mother Courage comes out.

COOK: Now don't make a scene . . .

MOTHER COURAGE (*coming out, laden with goods*): Yvette! (*They embrace.*) But why are you in mourning?

YVETTE: Doesn't it suit me? My husband, the colonel, died several years ago.

MOTHER COURAGE: The old fellow that nearly bought my wagon?

YVETTE: His elder brother.

MOTHER COURAGE: So you're not doing badly. Good to see one person who got somewhere in the war.

YVETTE: I've had my ups and downs.

MOTHER COURAGE: Don't let's speak ill of colonels. They make money like hay.

CHAPLAIN (*to the* COOK): If I were you, I'd put my shoes on again. (*To* YVETTE:) You promised to give us your opinion of this gentleman.

COOK: Now, Yvette, don't make a stink!

MOTHER COURAGE: He's a friend of mine, Yvette.

YVETTE: He's—Peter Piper, that's who.

MOTHER COURAGE: What!

COOK: Cut the nicknames. My name's Lamb.

MOTHER COURAGE (*laughing*): Peter Piper? Who turned the women's heads? And I've been keeping your pipe for you.

CHAPLAIN: And smoking it.

YVETTE: Lucky I can warn you against him. He's a bad lot. You won't find worse on the whole coast of Flanders. He got more girls in trouble than . . .

COOK: That's a long time ago, it isn't true any more.

YVETTE: Stand up when you talk to a lady! Oh, how I loved that man; and all the time he was having a little bowlegged brunette. He got *her* into trouble too, of course.

COOK: I seem to have brought *you* luck!

YVETTE: Shut your trap, you hoary ruin! And you take care, Mother Courage, this type is still dangerous even in decay!

MOTHER COURAGE (*to* YVETTE): Come with me, I must get rid of this stuff before the prices fall.

YVETTE (*concentrating on the* COOK): Miserable cur!

MOTHER COURAGE: Maybe you can help me at army headquarters, you have contacts.

YVETTE: Seducer!

MOTHER COURAGE (*shouting into the wagon*): Kattrin, church is all off, I'm going to market!

YVETTE: Whore hunter!

MOTHER COURAGE (*still to* KATTRIN): When Eilif comes, give him something to drink!

YVETTE: That a man like him should have been able to turn me from the straight and narrow! I have my own star to thank that I rose none the less to the heights! But I've put an end to your tricks, Peter Piper, and one day—in a better life than this—the Lord God will reward me! Come, Mother Courage! (*She leaves with* MOTHER COURAGE.)

CHAPLAIN: As our text this morning let us take the saying: the mills of God grind slowly. And you complain of my jokes!

COOK: I never have any luck. I'll be frank, I was hoping for a good hot dinner, I'm starving. And now they'll be talking about me, and she'll get a completely wrong picture. I think I should go before she comes back.

CHAPLAIN: I think so too.

COOK: Chaplain, peace makes me sick. Mankind must perish by fire and sword, we're born and bred in sin! Oh, how I wish I was roasting a great fat capon for the Commander—God knows where *he's* got to —with mustard sauce and those little yellow carrots . . .

CHAPLAIN: Red cabbage—with capon, red cabbage.

COOK: You're right. But he always wanted yellow carrots.

CHAPLAIN: He never understood a thing.

COOK: You always put plenty away.

CHAPLAIN: Under protest.

COOK: Anyway, you must admit, those were the days.

CHAPLAIN: Yes, that I might admit.

COOK: Now you've called her a hyena, there's not much future for you here either. What are you staring at?

CHAPLAIN: It's Eilif!

Followed by two soldiers with halberds, EILIF *enters. His hands are fettered. He is white as chalk.*

CHAPLAIN: What's happened to you?

EILIF: Where's mother?

CHAPLAIN: Gone to town.

EILIF: They said she was here. I was allowed a last visit.

COOK (*to the* SOLDIERS): Where are you taking him?

A SOLDIER: For a ride.

The other SOLDIER *makes the gesture of throat cutting.*

CHAPLAIN: What has he done?

SOLDIER: He broke in on a peasant. The wife is dead.

CHAPLAIN: Eilif, how could you?

EILIF: It's no different. It's what I did before.

COOK: That was in war time.

EILIF: Shut your hole. Can I sit down till she comes?

SOLDIER: No.

CHAPLAIN: It's true. In war time they honored him for it. He sat at the Commander's right hand. It was bravery. Couldn't we speak with the military police?

SOLDIER: What's the use? Stealing cattle from a peasant, what's brave about that?

COOK: It was just stupid.

EILIF: If I'd been stupid, I'd have starved, smarty.

COOK: So you were bright and paid for it.

CHAPLAIN: At least we must bring Kattrin out.

EILIF: Let her alone. Just give me some brandy.

SOLDIER: No.

CHAPLAIN: What shall we tell your mother?

EILIF: Tell her it was no different. Tell her it was the same. Oh, tell her nothing.

The SOLDIERS *take him away.*

CHAPLAIN: I'll come with you, I'll . . .

EILIF: I don't need a priest!

CHAPLAIN: You don't know—yet. (*He follows him.*)

COOK (*calling after him*): I'll have to tell her, she'll want to see him!

CHAPLAIN: Better tell her nothing. Or maybe just that he was here, and he'll return, maybe tomorrow. Meantime I'll be back and can break the news. (*He leaves quickly.*)

The COOK *looks after him, shakes his head, then walks about uneasily. Finally, he approaches the wagon.*

COOK: Hello! Won't you come out? You want to sneak
away from the peace, don't you? Well, so do I! I'm
the Swedish Commander's cook, remember me? I
was wondering if you've got anything to eat in
there—while we're waiting for your mother. I
wouldn't mind a bit of bacon—or even bread—just
to pass the time. (*He looks in.*) She's got a blanket
over her head.

The thunder of cannon.

MOTHER COURAGE *runs in, out of breath, still carrying the goods.*

MOTHER COURAGE: Cook, the peace is over, the war's on
again, has been for three days! I didn't get rid of this
stuff after all, thank God! There's a shooting match
in the town already—with the Lutherans. We must
get away with the wagon. Pack, Kattrin! What's on
your mind? Something the matter?

COOK: Nothing.

MOTHER COURAGE: But there is. I see it in your face.

COOK: Because the war's on again, most likely. May it
last till tomorrow evening, so I can get something in
my belly!

MOTHER COURAGE: You're not telling me.

COOK: Eilif was here. Only he had to go away again.

MOTHER COURAGE: He was here? Then we'll see him on
the march. I'll be with our side this time. How'd he
look?

COOK: The same.

MOTHER COURAGE: He'll *never* change. And the war
couldn't get *him*, he's bright. Help me with the
packing. (*She starts it.*) Did he tell you anything?
Is he well in with the Provost? Did he tell you about
his heroic deeds?

COOK (*darkly*): He's done one of them again.

MOTHER COURAGE: Tell me about it later. (KATTRIN *appears.*) Kattrin, the peace is over, we're on the move

again. (*To the* COOK:) What *is* the matter with you?

COOK: I'll enlist.

MOTHER COURAGE: A good idea. Where's the Chaplain?

COOK: In the town. With Eilif.

MOTHER COURAGE: Stay with us a while, Lamb, I need a bit of help.

COOK: This matter of Yvette . . .

MOTHER COURAGE: Hasn't done you any harm at all in my eyes. Just the opposite. Where there's smoke, there's fire, they say. You'll come?

COOK: I may as well.

MOTHER COURAGE: The Twelfth Regiment's under way. Into harness with you! Maybe I'll see Eilif before the day is out, just think! That's what I like best. Well, it wasn't such a long peace, we can't grumble. Let's go!

The COOK *and* KATTRIN *are in harness.*

MOTHER COURAGE *sings*:

> From Ulm to Metz, past dome and steeple
> My wagon always moves ahead.
> The war can care for all its people
> So long as there is steel and lead.
> Though steel and lead are stout supporters
> A war needs human beings too.
> Report today to your headquarters!
> If it's to last, this war needs you!

9

The great war of religion has lasted sixteen years and Germany has lost half its inhabitants. Those who are spared in battle die by plague. Over once blooming countryside hunger rages. Towns are burned down. Wolves prowl the empty streets. In the autumn of 1634 we find Mother Courage in the Fichtelgebirge not far from the road the Swedish army is taking. Winter has come early and is hard. Business is bad. Only begging remains. The cook receives a letter from Utrecht and is sent packing.

In front of a half-ruined parsonage. Early winter. A gray morning. Gusts of wind. MOTHER COURAGE *and the* COOK *at the wagon in shabby clothes.*

COOK: There are no lights on. No one's up.

MOTHER COURAGE: But it's a parsonage. The parson'll have to leave his feather bed and ring the bells. Then he'll have some hot soup.

COOK: Where'll he get it from? The whole village is starving.

MOTHER COURAGE: The house is lived in. There was a dog barking.

COOK: If the parson has anything, he'll hang on to it.

MOTHER COURAGE: Maybe if we sang him something . . .

COOK: I've had enough. (*Suddenly:*) I didn't tell you, a letter came from Utrecht. My mother's died of cholera, the inn is mine. There's the letter, if you don't believe me. I'll show it to you, though my aunt's railing about me and my ups and downs is none of your business.

MOTHER COURAGE (*reading*): Lamb, I'm tired of wander-

95

ing, too. I feel like a butcher's dog taking meat to my customers and getting none myself. I've nothing more to sell and people have nothing to pay with. In Saxony someone tried to force a chestful of books on me in return for two eggs. And in Württemberg they would have let me have their plough for a bag of salt. Nothing grows any more, only thorn bushes. In Pomerania I hear the villagers have been eating their younger children. Nuns have been caught committing robbery.

COOK: The world's dying out.

MOTHER COURAGE: Sometimes I see myself driving through hell with this wagon and selling brimstone. And sometimes I'm driving through heaven handing our provisions to wandering souls! If only we could find a place where there's no shooting, me and my children—what's left of 'em—we might rest a while.

COOK: We could open this inn together. Think about it, Courage. *My* mind's made up. With or without you, I'm leaving for Utrecht. And today too.

MOTHER COURAGE: I must talk to Kattrin, it's a bit sudden, and I don't like to make my decisions in the cold on an empty stomach. (KATTRIN *emerges from the wagon.*) Kattrin, I've something to tell you. The cook and I want to go to Utrecht, he's been left an inn. You'd be able to stay put and get to know some people. Many a man'd be prepared to take on a girl with a position. Looks aren't everything. I like the idea. I get on well with the cook. I'll say this for him: he has a head for business. We'd be sure of our dinner, that would be all right, wouldn't it? You'd have your own bed, what do you think of *that*? In the long run, this is no life, on the road. You might be killed any time. You're eaten up with lice as it is. And we must decide now, because otherwise we go north with the Swedes. They must be over there somewhere. (*She points left.*) I think we'll decide to go, Kattrin.

COOK: Anna, I must have a word with you alone.

MOTHER COURAGE: Go back inside, Kattrin.

KATTRIN *does so.*

COOK: I'm interrupting because there's a misunderstanding, Anna. I thought I wouldn't have to say it right out, but I see I must. If you're bringing *her,* it's all off. Do we understand each other?
and is listening.

KATTRIN *has her head out of the back of the wagon*

MOTHER COURAGE: You mean I leave Kattrin behind?

COOK: What do you think? There's no room in the inn, it isn't one of those places with three counters. If the two of us look lively we can earn a living, but three's too many. Let Kattrin keep your wagon.

MOTHER COURAGE: I was thinking we might find her a husband in Utrecht.

COOK: Don't make me laugh. With that scar? And old as she is? And dumb?

MOTHER COURAGE: Not so loud!

COOK: Loud or soft, what is, is. That's another reason I can't have her in the inn. Customers don't like having something like that always before their eyes. You can't blame them.

MOTHER COURAGE: Shut up. I told you not to talk so loud.

COOK: There's a light in the parsonage, we can sing now!

MOTHER COURAGE: Cook, how could she pull the wagon by herself? The war frightens her. She can't bear it. She has terrible dreams. I hear her groan at night, especially after battles. What she sees in her dreams I don't know. She suffers from sheer pity. The other day I found her with a hedgehog that we'd run over.

COOK: The inn's too small. (*Calling:*) Worthy Sir, menials, and all within! We now present the song of Solomon, Julius Caesar, and other great souls who came to no good, so you can see we're law-abiding folk too, and have a hard time getting by, especially in winter.

He sings "The Song of the Great Souls of this Earth":

> King Solomon was very wise,
> So what's his history?
> He came to view this life with scorn,
> Yes, he came to regret he ever had been born
> Declaring: all is vanity.
> King Solomon was very wise,
> But long before the day was out
> The consequence was clear, alas:
> His wisdom 'twas that brought him to this pass.
> A man is better off without.

For the virtues are dangerous in this world, as our fine song tells. You're better off without, you have a nice life, breakfast included—some good hot soup maybe . . . I'm an example of a man who's not had any, and I'd like some, I'm a soldier, but what good did my bravery do me in all those battles? None at all. I might just as well have wet my pants like a poltroon and stayed at home. For why?

> Old Julius Caesar, he was brave.
> His fame shall never cease.
> He sat like a god on an altar piece.
> Yet they tore brave old Julius limb from valiant
>   limb
> And Brutus helped to slaughter him.
> Old Julius was very brave
> But long before the day was out
> The consequence was clear, alas:
> His bravery 'twas that brought him to this pass.
> A man is better off without.

(*Under his breath*:) They don't even look out. (*Aloud*:) Worthy Sir, menials, and all within! You could say, no, courage isn't the thing to fill a man's

belly, try honesty, that should be worth a dinner, at
any rate it must have *some* effect. Let's see.

> You all know honest Socrates
> Who always spoke the truth.
> They owed him thanks for that, you'd think,
> But what happened? Why, they put hemlock
>   in his drink
> And swore that he misled the youth.
> How honest was this Socrates!
> Yet long before the day was out
> The consequence was clear, alas:
> His honesty had brought him to this pass.
> A man is better off without.

Yes, we're told to be unselfish and share what we
have, but what if we have nothing? And those who
do share it don't have an easy time either, for what's
left when you're through sharing? Unselfishness is
a very rare virtue—it doesn't pay.

> Unselfish Martin could not bear
> His fellow creatures' woes.
> He met a poor man in the snows
> And he gave this poor fellow half his cloak to
>   wear:
> So both of them fell down and froze.
> His brothers' woes he could not bear,
> So long before the day was out
> The consequence was clear, alas:
> Unselfishness had brought him to this pass.
> A man is better off without.

That's how it is with us. We're law-abiding folk, we
keep to ourselves, don't steal, don't kill, don't burn
the place down. And in this way we sink lower and
lower and the song proves true and there's no soup
going. And if we were different, if we were thieves
and killers, maybe we could eat our fill! For virtues

bring no reward, only vices. Such is the world, need
it be so?

> God's ten commandments we have kept
> And acted as we should.
> It has not done us any good.
> All you people who sit beside a roaring fire
> O help us in our need so dire!
> The ten commandments we have kept
> And long before the day was out
> The consequence was clear, alas:
> Our godliness has brought us to this pass.
> A man is better off without.

VOICE (*from above*): You there! Come up! There's some
soup here for you!

MOTHER COURAGE: Lamb, I couldn't swallow a thing. I
don't say what you said is unreasonable, but was
it your last word? We've always understood each
other.

COOK: Yes, Anna. Think it over.

MOTHER COURAGE: There's nothing to think over. I'm
not leaving her here.

COOK: You're going to be silly, but what can I do? I'm
not inhuman, it's just that the inn's a small one. And
now we must go up, or there'll be nothing doing
here too, and we've been singing in the cold for
nothing.

MOTHER COURAGE: I'll fetch Kattrin.

COOK: Better stick something in your pocket for her.
If there are three of us, they'll get a shock.

Exeunt.

KATTRIN *clambers out of the wagon with a bundle.
She makes sure they are both gone. Then, on a
wagon wheel, she lays out a skirt of her mother's
and a pair of the cook's trousers side by side and
easy to see. She has just finished, and has picked
up her bundle, when* MOTHER COURAGE *returns.*

MOTHER COURAGE (*with a plate of soup*): Kattrin! Stay
   where you are, Kattrin! Where do you think you're
   going with that bundle? (*She examines the bundle.*)
   She's packed her things. Were you listening? I told
   him there was nothing doing, he can *have* Utrecht
   and his lousy inn, what would we want with a lousy
   inn? (*She sees the skirt and trousers.*) Oh, you're
   a stupid girl, Kattrin, what if I'd seen that and you
   gone? (*She takes hold of* KATTRIN *who is trying to
   leave.*) And don't think I've sent him packing on
   your account. It was the wagon. You can't part us,
   I'm too used to it, it was the wagon. Now we're
   leaving and we'll put the cook's things here
   where he'll find 'em, the stupid man. (*She clambers
   up and throws a couple of things down to go
   with the trousers.*) There! He's fired. The last
   man I'll take into *this* business! Now let's be going,
   you and me. This winter'll pass, like all the others.
   Get into harness, it looks like snow.

*They harness themselves to the wagon, turn it around,
and start out. A gust of wind. Enter the* COOK, *still
chewing. He sees his things.*

10

During the whole of 1635 Mother Courage and Kattrin pull the wagon along the roads of central Germany in the wake of the ever more tattered armies.

On the highway. MOTHER COURAGE *and* KATTRIN *are pulling the wagon. They come to a prosperous farmhouse. Someone inside is singing.*

VOICE:

> In March a bush we planted
> To make the garden gay.
> In June we were enchanted:
> A lovely rose was blooming
> The balmy air perfuming!
> Blest are they
> Who have gardens gay!
> In June we were enchanted.
>
> When snow falls helter-skelter
> And loudly blows the storm
> Our farmhouse gives us shelter.
> The winter's in a hurry
> But we've no cause to worry.
> We are warm
> In the midst of the storm!
> Our farmhouse gives us shelter.

MOTHER COURAGE *and* KATTRIN *have stopped to listen. Then they start out again.*

11

January, 1636. Catholic troops threaten the Protestant town of Halle. The stone begins to speak. Mother Courage loses her daughter and journeys onward alone. The war is not yet near its end.

The wagon, very far gone now, stands near a farmhouse with a straw roof. It is night. Out of the woods come a LIEUTENANT *and three* SOLDIERS *in full armor.*

LIEUTENANT: And there mustn't be a sound. If anyone yells, cut him down.

FIRST SOLDIER: But we'll have to knock—if we want a guide.

LIEUTENANT: Knocking's a natural noise, it's all right, could be a cow hitting the wall of the cowshed.

The SOLDIERS *knock at the farmhouse door. An* OLD PEASANT WOMAN *opens. A hand is clapped over her mouth. Two* SOLDIERS *enter.*

A MAN'S VOICE: What is it?

The SOLDIERS *bring out an* OLD PEASANT *and his son.*

LIEUTENANT (*pointing to the wagon on which* KATTRIN *has appeared*): There's one. (*A* SOLDIER *pulls her out.*) Is this everybody that lives here?

PEASANTS (*alternating*): That's our son. And that's a girl that can't talk. Her mother's in town buying up stocks because the shopkeepers are running away and selling cheap. They're canteen people.

LIEUTENANT: I'm warning you. Keep quiet. One sound and we'll crack you over the head with a pike. And I need someone to show us the path to the town.

(*He points to the* YOUNG PEASANT:) You! Come here!

YOUNG PEASANT: I don't know any path!

SECOND SOLDIER (*grinning*): He don't know any path!

YOUNG PEASANT: I don't help Catholics.

LIEUTENANT (*to the* SECOND SOLDIER): Let him feel your pike in his side.

YOUNG PEASANT (*forced to his knees, the pike at his throat*): I'd rather die!

SECOND SOLDIER (*again mimicking*): He'd rather die!

FIRST SOLDIER: I know how to change his mind. (*He walks over to the cowshed.*) Two cows and a bull. Listen, you. If you aren't going to be reasonable, I'll saber your cattle.

YOUNG PEASANT: Not the cattle!

PEASANT WOMAN (*weeping*): Spare the cattle, Captain, or we'll starve!

LIEUTENANT: If he must be pigheaded!

FIRST SOLDIER: I think I'll start with the bull.

YOUNG PEASANT (*to the old one*): Do I have to? (*The older one nods.*) I'll do it.

PEASANT WOMAN: Thank you, thank you, Captain, for sparing us, for ever and ever, Amen.

The OLD MAN *stops her going on thanking him.*

FIRST SOLDIER: I knew the bull came first all right!

Led by the YOUNG PEASANT, *the* LIEUTENANT *and the* SOLDIERS *go on their way.*

OLD PEASANT: I wish we knew what it was. Nothing good, I suppose.

PEASANT WOMAN: Maybe they're just scouts. What are you doing?

OLD PEASANT (*setting a ladder against the roof and climbing up*): I'm seeing if they're alone. (*On the roof.*) Things are moving—all over. I can see armor. And cannon. There must be more than a regiment. God have mercy on the town and all within!

PEASANT WOMAN: Are there lights in the town?

OLD PEASANT: No, they're all asleep. (*He climbs down.*) There'll be an attack, and they'll all be slaughtered in their beds.

PEASANT WOMAN: The watchman'll give warning.

OLD PEASANT: They must have killed the watchman in the tower on the hill or he'd have sounded his horn before this.

PEASANT WOMAN: If there were more of us . . .

OLD PEASANT: But being that we're alone with that cripple . . .

PEASANT WOMAN: There's nothing we can do, is there?

OLD PEASANT: Nothing.

PEASANT WOMAN: We can't get down there. In the dark.

OLD PEASANT: The whole hillside's swarming with 'em.

PEASANT WOMAN: We could give a sign?

OLD PEASANT: And be cut down for it?

PEASANT WOMAN: No, there's nothing we can do. (*To* KATTRIN:) Pray, poor thing, pray! There's nothing we can do to stop this bloodshed, so even if you can't talk, at least pray! He hears, if no one else does. I'll help you. (*All kneel,* KATTRIN *behind.*) Our Father, which art in Heaven, hear our prayer, let not the town perish with all that lie therein asleep and fearing nothing. Wake them, that they rise and go the walls and see the foe that comes with fire and sword in the night down the hill and across the fields. (*Back to* KATTRIN:) God protect our mother and make the watchman not sleep but wake ere it's too late. And save our son-in-law, too, O God, he's there with his four children, let them not perish, they're innocent, they know nothing —(*To* KATTRIN, *who groans*:)—one of them's not two years old, the eldest is seven. (KATTRIN *rises, troubled.*) Heavenly Father, hear us, only Thou canst help us or we die, for we are weak and have no sword nor nothing; we cannot trust our own strength but only Thine, O Lord; we are in Thy hands, our cattle, our farm, and the town too, we're all in Thy hands, and the foe is nigh unto the walls with all his power.

KATTRIN, *unperceived, has crept off to the wagon, has taken something out of it, put it under her apron, and has climbed up the ladder to the roof.*

Be mindful of the children in danger, especially the little ones, be mindful of the old folk who cannot move, and of all Christian souls, O Lord.

OLD PEASANT: And forgive us our trespasses as we forgive them that trespass against us. Amen.

Sitting on the roof, KATTRIN *takes a drum from under her apron and starts to beat it.*

PEASANT WOMAN: Heavens, what's she doing?
OLD PEASANT: She's out of her mind!
PEASANT WOMAN: Get her down, quick.

The OLD PEASANT *runs to the ladder but* KATTRIN *pulls it up on the roof.*

She'll get us in trouble.
OLD PEASANT: Stop it this minute, you silly cripple!
PEASANT WOMAN: The soldiers'll come!
OLD PEASANT (*looking for stones*): I'll stone you!
PEASANT WOMAN: Have you no pity, have you no heart? We have relations there too, four grandchildren, but there's nothing we can do. If they find us now, it's the end, they'll stab us to death!

KATTRIN *is staring into the far distance, toward the town. She goes on drumming.*

PEASANT WOMAN (*to the* PEASANT): I told you not to let that riffraff on your farm. What do *they* care if we lose our cattle?
LIEUTENANT (*running back with* SOLDIERS *and the* YOUNG PEASANT): I'll cut you all to bits!

PEASANT WOMAN: We're innocent, sir, there's nothing we can do. She did it, a stranger!

LIEUTENANT: Where's the ladder?

OLD PEASANT: On the roof.

LIEUTENANT (*calling*): Throw down the drum. I order you! (KATTRIN *goes on drumming.*) You're all in this, but you won't live to tell the tale.

OLD PEASANT: They've been cutting down fir trees around here. If we bring a tall enough trunk we can knock her off the roof . . .

FIRST SOLDIER (*to the* LIEUTENANT): I beg leave to make a suggestion. (*He whispers something to the* LIEUTENANT, *who nods.*) Listen, you! We have an idea—for your own good. Come down and go with us to the town. Show us your mother and we'll spare her.

KATTRIN *goes on drumming.*

LIEUTENANT (*pushing him away*): She doesn't trust you, no wonder with your face. (*He calls up to* KATTRIN:) Hey, you! Suppose I give you my word? I'm an officer, my word's my bond!

KATTRIN *drums harder.*

Nothing is sacred to her.

YOUNG PEASANT: Sir, it's not just because of her mother!

FIRST SOLDIER: This can't go on, they'll hear it in the town as sure as hell.

LIEUTENANT: We must make another noise with something. Louder than that drum. What can we make a noise with?

FIRST SOLDIER: But we mustn't make a noise!

LIEUTENANT: A harmless noise, fool, a peacetime noise!

OLD PEASANT: I could start chopping wood.

LIEUTENANT: That's it! (*The* PEASANT *brings his ax and chops away.*) Chop! Chop harder! Chop for your life!

KATTRIN *has been listening, beating the drum less*

hard. Very upset, and peering around, she now goes on drumming.

It's not enough. (*To the* FIRST SOLDIER:) You chop too!

OLD PEASANT: I've only one ax. (*He stops chopping.*)

LIEUTENANT: We must set fire to the farm. Smoke her out.

OLD PEASANT: That's no good, Captain. When they see fire from the town, they'll know everything.

During the drumming KATTRIN *has been listening again. Now she laughs.*

LIEUTENANT: She's laughing at us, that's too much, I'll have her guts if it's the last thing I do. Bring a musket!

Two SOLDIERS *off.* KATTRIN *goes on drumming.*

PEASANT WOMAN: I have it, Captain. That's their wagon over there, Captain. If we smash that, she'll stop. It's all they have, Captain.

LIEUTENANT (*to the* YOUNG PEASANT): Smash it! (*Calling:*) If you don't stop that noise, we'll smash your wagon!

The YOUNG PEASANT *deals the wagon a couple of feeble blows with a board.*

PEASANT WOMAN (*to* KATTRIN): Stop, you little beast!

KATTRIN *stares at the wagon and pauses. Noises of distress come out of her. But she goes on drumming.*

LIEUTENANT: Where are those sons of bitches with that gun?

FIRST SOLDIER: They can't have heard anything in the town or we'd hear their cannon.

LIEUTENANT (*calling*): They don't hear you. And now we're going to shoot you. I'll give you one more chance: throw down that drum!

YOUNG PEASANT (*dropping the board, screaming to* KAT-

TRIN): Don't stop now! Or they're all done for. Go on, go on, go on . . .

The SOLDIER *knocks him down and beats him with his pike.* KATTRIN *starts crying but goes on drumming.*

PEASANT WOMAN: Not in the back, you're killing him!

The SOLDIERS *arrive with the musket.*

SECOND SOLDIER: The Colonel's foaming at the mouth. We'll be court-martialed.

LIEUTENANT: Set it up! Set it up! (*Calling while the musket is set up on forks:*) Once and for all: stop that drumming!

Still crying, KATTRIN *is drumming as hard as she can.*

Fire!

The SOLDIERS *fire.* KATTRIN *is hit. She gives the drum another feeble beat or two, then slowly collapses.*

LIEUTENANT: That's an end to the noise.

But the last beats of the drum are lost in the din of cannon from the town. Mingled with the thunder of cannon, alarm bells are heard in the distance.

FIRST SOLDIER: She made it.

12

*Toward morning. The drums and pipes of troops on the
march, receding. In front of the wagon* MOTHER COURAGE
sits by KATTRIN'S *body. The* PEASANTS *of the last scene
are standing near.*

PEASANTS: You must leave, woman. There's only one regiment to go. You can never get away by yourself.

MOTHER COURAGE: Maybe she's fallen asleep.

She sings:

Lullaby, baby, what's that in the hay?
The neighbor's kids cry but mine are gay.
The neighbor's kids are dressed in dirt:
Your silks are cut from an angel's skirt.
They are all starving: you have a pie.
If it's too stale, you need only cry.
Lullaby, baby, what's rustling there?
One lad fell in Poland. The other is—where?

You shouldn't have told her about the children.

PEASANTS: If you hadn't gone off to the town to get your
cut, maybe it wouldn't have happened.

MOTHER COURAGE: She's asleep now.

PEASANTS: She's not asleep, it's time you realized. She's
gone. You must get away. There are wolves in these
parts. And the bandits are worse.

MOTHER COURAGE: That's right. (*She goes and fetches a
cloth from the wagon to cover up the body.*)

PEASANT WOMAN: Have you no one now? Someone you
can go to?

MOTHER COURAGE: There's one. My Eilif.

PEASANT (*while* MOTHER COURAGE *covers the body*):

110

Find him then. Leave *her* to us. We'll give her a
proper burial. You needn't worry.

MOTHER COURAGE: Here's money for the expenses.

She pays the PEASANT. *The* PEASANT *and his son
shake her hand and carry* KATTRIN *away.*

PEASANT WOMAN (*also taking her hand, and bowing, as
she goes away*): Hurry!

MOTHER COURAGE (*harnessing herself to the wagon*): I
hope I can pull the wagon by myself. Yes, I'll man-
age, there's not much in it now. I must get back into
business.

*Another regiment passes at the rear with pipe and
drum.*

MOTHER COURAGE *starts pulling the wagon.*

MOTHER COURAGE: Hey! Take me with you!

Soldiers are heard singing:

> Dangers, surprises, devastations!
> The war moves on, but will not quit.
> And though it last three generations,
> We shall get nothing out of it.
> Starvation, filth, and cold enslave us.
> The army robs us of our pay.
> But God may yet come down and save us:
> His holy war won't end today.
> > Christians, awake! Winter is gone!
> > The snows depart! Dead men sleep on!
> > Let all of you who still survive
> > Get out of bed and look alive!

EDITORIAL NOTES

Mother Courage and Her Children was copyrighted in the U.S. in 1940, and first published here, not in German, but in English, in 1941: the translation was by H. R. Hays, and the play appeared in an anthology of new writing entitled *New Directions, 1941,* published by New Directions. An Eric Bentley version of the play, with the cuts made by Brecht for the German production, appeared in *The Modern Theatre,* volume two (Doubleday, Anchor, 1955). A second Bentley version, even more heavily cut for a projected American production, appeared in *Seven Plays by Bertolt Brecht* (Grove Press, 1961).

The world première of the play (and this *was* in German) took place in 1941 at the Zürich Schauspielhaus; the director was Leopold Lindtberg.

The now famous production of the Berliner Ensemble dates back to 1949 when Erich Engel and Bertolt Brecht put the play on at the Deutsches Theater in Berlin with Helene Weigel (Mrs. Bertolt Brecht) in the title role. When the play was last given (1960), Frau Weigel was one of the few performers from the original cast who was still in the show.

Professional productions of the play, adapted by Eric Bentley, have been staged in London (Unity Theatre and The National Theatre), Bristol (Old Vic), Dublin, Cleveland, New York, San Francisco, Winnipeg, and other cities. It has also been presented on BBC-Television.

The music to the world première in Zürich was by Paul Burkhard, and there is an as yet unused score by Darius Milhaud, composed expressly for English lyrics of Eric Bentley, but the music generally associated with the play is that of Paul Dessau, for which the lyrics in the present text were written. Part of Dessau's score can be heard, with the words in French, on a Vanguard Record (VRS-9022); part with the words sung in German by the Berlin cast, on East German records usually available from VEB Deutsche Schallplatten, Reichstagufer 4/5, Berlin W. 8. Two lyrics from the play, one set by Dessau, the other by Hanns Eisler, are to be found in the album *Bentley on Brecht* (Folkways Records, FH 5434).

Brecht's own scene-by-scene commentary on the play is to be found under the title "Brecht's Notes to *Mother Courage and Her Children*" in the British theatre magazine *Encore,* Number 55, May-June 1965, as translated by Eric Bentley and Hugo Schmidt.

AUTHOR'S NOTES TO
MOTHER COURAGE AND HER CHILDREN

The world première of *Mother Courage and Her Children* in Zürich during the Hitler War, with the outstanding Therese Giehse in the title role, made it possible, despite the antifascist and pacifist stand of the Zürich Schauspielhaus (mainly staffed with German emigrants), for the bourgeois press to speak of a Niobe tragedy and of the overwhelming vital strength of the mother animal. Duly warned, the playwright made some changes for the Berlin production. The original text follows.

From Scene One, pages 32-33

MOTHER COURAGE: . . . all of you: be careful, you'll need to be. Now let's climb on the wagon and move on.

SERGEANT: I don't feel very well.

RECRUITING OFFICER: Maybe you caught a chill when you handed over your helmet in all this wind.

The SERGEANT *grabs his helmet.*

MOTHER COURAGE: And you give me my papers. Someone else might ask for them and I'll be without. (*She collects them in her tin.*)

RECRUITING OFFICER (*to* EILIF): You can at least take a look at the boots. And we can have a drink, just us men. I can advance you money: come behind the wagon, and I'll prove it.

They go behind the wagon.

SERGEANT: I don't understand. I always stay in the rear. There's no safer spot for a sergeant to be. You can send the others on ahead in quest of fame. My appetite is ruined. I can tell you right now, I won't be able to get anything done.

MOTHER COURAGE (*going over to him*): You shouldn't take on so, just because you can't eat. Just stay in the rear. Here, take a slug of brandy, man, and no offense. (*She gives him something to drink from the wagon.*)

RECRUITING OFFICER (*who has taken* EILIF's *arm and is making off toward the back*): You die anyway. You drew a cross, so what? Ten guilders in advance and you're a soldier of the king and a stout fellow and the women will be mad about you. And you can give me a smack in the puss for insulting you.

Both leave. Dumb KATTRIN *lets out harsh cries, for she has seen the abduction.*

MOTHER COURAGE: Coming, Kattrin, coming. The Sergeant isn't well, he's superstitious, I didn't know that. And now we'll be going. Where's Eilif?

SWISS CHEESE: He must have gone with the recruiting officer. He was talking with him the whole time.

From Scene Five, pages 70-72

MOTHER COURAGE: What, you can't pay? No money, no brandy! They can play victory marches, they should pay their men!

SOLDIER (*threateningly*): I want my brandy! I arrived too late for plunder. The Chief allowed one hour for plunder. He's not inhuman, he says. So I suppose they bought him off.

The CHAPLAIN *staggers in.*

CHAPLAIN: There are more in the farmhouse. A family of peasants. Help me, someone, I need linen!

The SECOND SOLDIER *goes off with him.*

MOTHER COURAGE: I have none. I sold all my bandages to the regiment. I'm not tearing up my officers' shirts for these people.

CHAPLAIN (*calling back*): I said I need linen!

MOTHER COURAGE (*rummaging around in her wagon*): Not a thing! They have nothing, and they pay nothing!

The CHAPLAIN *stoops over a* WOMAN *whom he has brought on.*

CHAPLAIN: Why did you stay out there in the line of fire?

WOMAN (*weakly*): Our farm . . .

MOTHER COURAGE: Expect *them* to leave? My beautiful shirts. My officers will be coming tomorrow, and I won't have a thing for them. (*She throws some stuff down.* KATTRIN *takes it to the* PEASANT WOMAN.) What am I doing, giving stuff away? I didn't start the war.

FIRST SOLDIER: They're Protestants. Why should they be Protestants?

MOTHER COURAGE: Protestant, Catholic, what do *they* care? Their farm's gone, that's what.

SECOND SOLDIER: They're not Protestants anyway: they're Catholics.

FIRST SOLDIER: In a bombardment we can't pick and choose.

A PEASANT *is brought in by the* CHAPLAIN.

PEASANT: My arm's gone.

From the house comes the cry of a child in pain.

CHAPLAIN (*to the* PEASANT WOMAN): Don't get up.

MOTHER COURAGE: Get the child out of there.

KATTRIN *runs off.*

MOTHER COURAGE (*tearing up shirts*): Half a guilder a

shirt. I'm ruined. Don't move her when you're bandaging, it may be her back. (*To* KATTRIN *who has
brought a young baby out of the ruins and is rocking
it as she walks around*:) Another baby to drag around
—you must be pleased with yourself! Give it to its
mother this minute. Or do I have to fight you again
for hours till I get it from you? Are you deaf? (KAT-
TRIN *ignores all this*.) I have nothing but losses from
your victories. Now, make do with this, Chaplain,
don't waste any of my linen, do you hear?

CHAPLAIN: I need more. The blood's coming through.

MOTHER COURAGE (*referring to* KATTRIN): There she sits,
happy as a lark in all this misery. Give the baby
back, the mother is coming to! (*As* KATTRIN *finally
and reluctantly gives the child back to the* PEASANT
WOMAN, MOTHER COURAGE *rips up a new shirt*.) I'm
giving nothing, I *can* give nothing, I have myself to
think of. (*To the* SECOND SOLDIER:) Don't stand
around gawking, go back there and tell them to stop
that music, I can see their victory without it. Have
yourself a glass of brandy, Chaplain, don't say no, I
have enough to cope with. (*She has to get down from
the wagon to snatch her daughter from the* FIRST
SOLDIER, *who is drunk*.) You beast! You want another
victory, do you? Well, you don't get away from me
without paying up! (*To the* PEASANT:) Your child
is all right. (*Pointing to the* WOMAN:) Get something down her. (*To the* FIRST SOLDIER:) Then leave
this coat. It's stolen goods anyhow.

FIRST SOLDIER *staggers away.* MOTHER COURAGE *goes
on ripping shirts.*

CHAPLAIN: There's still someone in there.

MOTHER COURAGE: Don't worry, I'll tear up all I have.

From Scene Seven, page 82

A highway, The CHAPLAIN, MOTHER COURAGE, *and* KAT-TRIN *pull the wagon. It is dirty and neglected, but new wares are hanging from it.*

MOTHER COURAGE (*sings*):
> So many seek a bed to sleep in:
> Each ditch is taken, and each cave,
> And he who seeks a hole to creep in
> Finds he has dug an early grave.
> And many a man spends many a minute.
> In hurrying toward some resting place.
> You wonder, when at last he's in it,
> Just why the fellow forced the pace.

She plays the refrain, "Christians, awake!" *on the harmonica.*

From Scene Twelve, page 110

PEASANTS: You must leave, woman. There's only one regiment to go. You can never get away by yourself.
MOTHER COURAGE: She's still breathing. Maybe she's fallen asleep.

Of the Peasants' War, which was the greatest misfortune of German history, one may say that, socially considered, it pulled the teeth of the Reformation. Its legacy was cynicism and business as usual. Mother Courage (let it be said to help performances in the theatre) recognizes, as do her friends and guests and nearly everyone, the purely commercial character of the war: this is precisely what attracts her. She believes in the war to the end. It never occurs to her that one must have a big pair of scissors to take one's cut out of a war. Those who look on at catastrophes wrongly expect those involved to learn something. So long as the masses are the *object* of politics they cannot regard what happens to them as an experiment but only as a fate. They learn as little from catastrophe as a scientist's rabbit learns of biology. It is not incumbent on the playwright to give Mother Courage insight at the end— she sees something, around the middle of the play, at the close of the sixth scene, then loses again what she has seen—his concern is that the spectator should see.

—B.B.

APPENDIX
THE SOURCES OF *MOTHER COURAGE*

There are three principal documents to consult. Two of them are currently available as paperbacks, notably, Grimmelshausen's *The Adventurous Simplicissimus* (Bison Book 134) and the same author's *The Runagate Courage* (Bison Book 300). The third is a ballad from J. L. Runeberg's *Songs of Ensign Stål* (*Fänrik Ståls Sägner*, Canto XXII). A translation of this ballad is given here in its entirety.*

LOTTA SVÄRD

At evening often it happens yet,
    When the genial hearth we guard,
That a veteran old from the war is met,
    And we chat about Lotta Svärd.

Though sullen the man may have been before,
    More kindly his face now grows,
And his gray moustache doth a curl come o'er,
    And a smile on his visage grows.

He thinks how oft from the battle-plain,
    From victory's field all spent
And wearied, came he a glass to drain,
    In Lotta's rickety tent.

And with pleasure he speaks of the woman then,—
    A word in a laughing mood;
But he darker grows when you laugh again,
    If your laugh is not glad and good.

For a pearl on the pathway of war was she,

---

* From *Songs of Ensign Stål* translated by Clement Burbank Shaw. New York: G. E. Stechert, 1925.

121

And a pearl all genuine, too:
Though sometimes laughable she might be,
    More oft was honor her due.

And did youth and beauty still round her cling?
    She reckoned of years a score
Since Third Gustavus was Sweden's king,
    When blossoms her spring-time wore.

Ere that noble monarch in Finland fought,
    Became she a warrior's bride;
When the drum called Svärd as a patriot,
    She followed it at his side.

She then was pretty. You scarce could find
    A lip or a cheek so fair;
And many a warrior had gazed him blind
    On her brown eyes' radiance rare.

But a spring is fleeting, a blooming brief,
    Not long lived her vernal prime;
In three transitions it came to grief,—
    A third at each single time.

One left with the first of winter's cold,
    Sent early, but long-careered;
The next was the theft of the summer bold,
    By withering sun-rays seared.

One part, the third, that till then had stood,
    She held but in slight regard;
She let it drown in her tear-drops' flood,
    When he fell in the conflict, Svärd.

When the last war broke with its wild alarms,
    And again she was midst us shown,
She scarce could recall when decayed her charms,
    So long, long ago they had flown.

But beauty yet, though in other ways,
    To a warrior's thought she bore,

And often still she was named with praise,
    As in years the most flowery of yore;—

Though her smiles' headquarters, so fair once known
    Now housed of wrinkles a train,
And brown no more was her eye alone,
    But her features' entire domain.

She loved the war, whatsoe'er it brought,—
    If weal, woe, trouble or cheer;
And the gray-clad boys had her tenderest thought,
    And so she to us was dear.

And had any with Svärd by his flag stood brave,
    He was sure not to be forgot;
To such one ampler the measure she gave,
    And for this became praise her lot.

She followed the army, so brave and true,
    Where'er on its march it strayed,
And where shots resounded and bullets flew,
    Never far behind she stayed.

And the dear young soldiers' heroic mood
    She loved in its full display,
And thought, howe'er near to the strife she stood,
    That she was not nearer than they!

And if one sank weary, in smoke and fire,
    Or received an all-glorious wound,
To station her shop, was her sole desire,
    Where a "strengthener" quick was found.

And the old gray tent it revealed to view,
    If one to the lappet should look,
That it once had harbored a bullet or two,
    And some pride in these patrons she took.

Now listen kindly, and hear my lay,
    For ne'er did I see her again:

'Twas ended,—Oravais' bloody day,—
    And we were retreating then.

And she was there, barely saved her part
    From battle, her only store,—
Her tent, her measure, her bucket and cart,
    And her gray horse spavined and sore.

We halted. Her stock did Lotta disclose,
    Kept bar on her wonted line;
Her tent discarding, the roof she chose
    Was now but a lofty pine.

And she was downcast, although full oft
    With a laugh she dissembled yet;
She mourned for the brave boys' woe, and she laughed,
    But her dark-brown cheek it was wet.

Then came, approaching her, where she stood,
    An arrogant young dragoon;
His glance revealed a presumptuous mood,
    And of self resounded his tone:

"Pour out!" he ordered, "Nor fearful blink!
    To-night I will pay the bill;
For I have silver, you hear it clink,
    And friends I can touch at will!"

A glance of disdain at the snob she sent:
    "Very well, I've measured your way;
For a needy mother to war you went,
    But how much have you fought this day?

"In my tent faint-hearted you sat, and weak,
    Complained of a wound to-day;
You now have color, then pale your cheek,
    And where does the wound lie, pray?

"Say not that your mother the grave doth hold,
    That not for her have you fought;

For lo, this land is your mother old,—
    And fraud to this mother you've brought.

"And had you of treasures your knapsack full,
    And could draw them from seas o'errun,
Despite your gold not a drop I'd pull,
    By God, for so base a son!"

And at her side she but clenched her fist,
    In her wonted manner so queer;
And the rich young stormer did not persist
    In trying to come more near.

But by the roadside, not far away,
    A youth was sitting alone;
On him did her pitying glances stray
    Like the mildest of starlight known.

It seemed, if upon him you looked again,
    Where his gun to support him stood,
That our hastening march he had followed in pain,
    And his coat was imbrued with blood.

Upon him turned she her eyes anon,
    So mother-like, warm and kind,
As if every glass for a customer drawn
    Were only for him designed.

But when gradual sank he lower and lower
    In the mournful visions that came,
She seemed to grow weary of waiting more,
    And she murmured the young man's name.

"Come," thus she spoke with a broken voice,
    "Here yet is a drop, indeed!
Come here, my boy, in a draught rejoice;
    It is solace we all now need.

"You shrink? What more then! Full well I know
    That you have in your knapsack no gold;—

You have come from forest to meet the foe,
    And gold not here could you mold.

"But no coward, you, when required was your
                                  blood,—
    This saw I on Lappo's plain;
At Ruona first on the bridge you stood,
    When 'twas stormed,—can you see it again?

"Regret it not, if a glass you claim;
    May a recompense in it swim;
One glass for Lappo, in gratitude's name,
    For Ruona, two to the brim!

"And stood he, Svärd, and his gun yet bore,
    With his kind and valorous soul,
And saw to-day how you gave once more
    Your body and blood as toll,—

"Then standing beside him would you be found
    As a son by the side of his sire,
And as sure as I live, through the world around,
    No pair would be more to admire!"

The soldier came, and her glass she filled
    For the brave, to the uppermost brim;
And chance for good measure she also distilled
    Two tear-drops therein for him.

It is long ago since I saw her face,
    Yet doth she in my memory dwell;
And the woman's story I gladly retrace,
    And all she has merited well.

For a pearl on the pathway of war was she,
    And a pearl all genuine, too;
Though sometimes laughable she might be,
    More oft was honor her due.